My Own Story

Donahue

by Phil Donahue & Co.

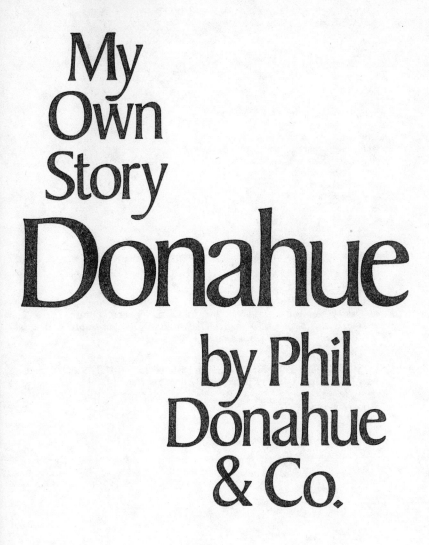

Simon and Schuster
New York

Photo editor: Vincent Virga
Manufactured in the United States of America

The authors are grateful for permission to reprint the following excerpts:
From Oakley Haldeman, Al Trace and Jimmy Lee's song, "Brush Those Tears
from Your Eyes," page 10, © 1948 MCA Music, A Division of MCA, Inc., New
York, New York. Used by permission. All rights reserved.

From Mike Chapman and Nicky Chinn's song, "Kiss You All Over," page 97,
© 1979 Chinnichap Publishing, Inc. Administered in the U.S.A. and Canada by
Careers Music, Inc. Used by permission. All rights reserved.

For my children,
Mike, Kev, Dan, Jim, and Mary Rose,
Who taught me things I should have known.

And for Marlo,
Who taught me things I thought I knew.

Donahue

1
Celebrity

IF I could start parenthood over again—and I wish I could—the biggest change I'd make is in stroking. Out loud. When my kids pleased me, I never told them so. Children get criticized, and pushed and pulled as though they were clay, to be molded (and spanked) into praiseworthy adults reflecting the virtues of their parents. On more than one occasion, I have surveyed my studio audience on the issue of spanking, and in all shows of hands, it wins.

My own view of this has changed; unfortunately for my kids, the change came too late. I believe it is difficult to get through parenthood without spanking (especially in homes with many children); however, I believe the *ideal* is never to spank. I am surprised by the majority of parents who disagree and see corporal punishment as a necessary feature of responsible parenthood.

Spanking and verbal criticism have become, to many parents, more important tools of child rearing than approval. We should not be surprised that countless young men and women enter adulthood with negative feelings about themselves. No wonder positive reenforcement is so often lacking in the relationships between boss and subordinate, teacher and student. Comic Rodney Dangerfield is not alone in complaining about "no respect," and what is not so funny is that this human condition may be the rule rather than the exception.

Amid these slump-shouldered victims of criticism (who are about the business of fulfilling the prophecy) come a select few mortals who have the opposite problem: *too much approval.*

There is a name for this rare species. A name which is not always given to geniuses, which most millionaires can't buy and which untold numbers of people covet, but will never have. Against million-to-one odds, I've got it.

It is called celebrity.

Celebrities fall somewhere between Sinatra and the weekend TV weatherman. One of the fascinating features of being a celebrity is trying to figure out where you are between the two. At first, I thoroughly enjoyed being famous. Then I began to analyze it. It started when a Delta Airlines co-pilot came out of the cockpit and asked for my autograph. He may never know how impressed I was. Then I hit the really big time when Ed Sudol asked me for my autograph at Wrigley Field before a Chicago Cubs baseball game. Sudol is a major-league umpire! Now, that's *big!* But my all-time great autograph experience came one night in Boston. Carl Yastrzemski, one of baseball's all-timers, asked me for *my* autograph, for his wife.

In Dayton, a teen-age employee of the Cassano Pizza chain refused to let me pay for a "large with everything." Embarrassed, I said, "Thanks, but I'd really like to pay." He was adamant, and I got a free pizza. Welfare mothers would pay; Phil Donahue gets his free!

With minimal effort, a celebrity in Chicago could go for weeks without picking up a check, and some do. It is one way restaurants advertise. There are four columnists in Chicago who will tell you that it is Liza Minnelli's birthday, and it is also their tradition to report which biggies ate where, and—as restaurateurs in Chicago know—a one-liner in a gossip column can boost business noticeably.

I recently took my son Kevin and his red 1971 Camaro to a Chevrolet dealer on the North Shore in suburban Chicago. The car wasn't shifting into third gear. We walked in, and a man with his name on his shirt came over and said, "What can I do for you?"

"My son's got a problem with his Camaro, Bob. It doesn't shift into third gear," I say, knowing the man does not recognize me. (Celebrities become expert at sensing nonrecognition.) I am upset, because my high visibility is the reason I have accompanied Kevin. I thought I would be insurance against exploitation.

"Boy, that's the transmission, all right," he says, shaking his head. "It'll be three hundred ninety-five dollars."

"Wait a minute; how do you know?"

"Because it's the transmission, and the transmission costs three ninety-five," he says.

"You don't even know what color the car is; you haven't even seen the car. I have the feeling you are not really interested in helping me solve the problem," I argued.

"No, it's not that; it's just that any dealer will tell you when you talk about the transmission, if we have to go into that transmission, it's three hundred ninety-five dollars."

"How do you know you have to go into the transmission?"

"You said it isn't shifting into third."

"Right, but you can't just assume—"

Just then a man in a suit and tie approaches and says, like a bad actor, "We can help *Mr. Donahue* here, right?" Kevin is watching and listening as the white-collar guy says to Bob, "Why not take the car around the block and I'll wait here with *Mr. Donahue?*"

Bob and Kevin leave for the test drive, and I am thinking about the poor soul who comes here and has the severe handicap of not having his own TV show.

Mr. Big says, "Are your shows live over there at WGN?"

"Do you realize that automobile dealers have the worst image of any business in the entire free world?" I say. "And what has just happened here is one of the reasons why?"

"Yeah," Mr. Big says, hangdog, "but we're working on it."

"You didn't want to fix my son's car. All you want to do is make three hundred ninety-five dollars. C'mon!"

Kevin and Bob return, and our instructions are to come back at 5:30. Kevin goes to the dealership at 5:30 and drives home to announce that his car shifts into third and there was *no charge*. My oldest son, Michael, wants to know if I'll go with him when his car needs repair, and I am feeling guilty.

Now, what should I do about this? Do I go back? I should go back and say, "I don't want this free; I want to pay for whatever you did to fix the car." Ralph Nader would have gone back with three investigators and a Polaroid camera and effectively scared the hell out of this merchant, increasing the chances that regular folk would receive fair treatment from this fast shuffler.

But Kevin is home; his car works fine; it didn't cost anything and besides, the repair department at the dealership would probably be closed by now. I do nothing. Score one more for cronyism and celebrity ass kissing in Chicago!

Airlines are interesting. They not only favor celebrities; they court them. I have often been asked if I wanted to board early (which I declined), and on more than one occasion I have been invited to first class from coach while in flight (which I accepted).

During an appearance of Eastern Air Lines President Frank Borman on *Donahue,* I did a big song-and-dance on the foolishness of paying twice as much for first class when "the front and back parts of the plane arrive at the same time." "Do you realize it costs *twice* as much to fly first class?" I ask incredulously.

"Some people like it," Borman says.

"They're suckers," I say grandly.

When I fly with my sons, I fly coach. However—and here's the embarrassing part: I notice that I miss first class. Intellectually, I think it is a gross waste of money, but emotionally, I like it. Am I becoming a spoiled celebrity?

On a personal vacation trip to St. Maarten, I am flying Eastern and I am in first class. The crew and stewardesses recognize me, and later, as I lie in the sun on the beach in the Netherlands Antilles, I have a mental picture of Frank Borman reading a memo from the crew on my flight and saying out loud, "Why, that S.O.B.!"

I tip like crazy. I am very self-conscious about this. I reason that when my party exits the restaurant, the only patron they'll remember is me. Big tip! Celebrity can be expensive.

Six years ago when Mike Douglas appeared on my show in Dayton, I was very impressed by the fact that he was accompanied by one vice-president and two "gofers." Dinah, during her visit to my program, was surrounded by five people, all men. Suddenly I notice I am uncomfortable traveling alone. What's the reason for this? What kind of support do I need? I notice I seldom shop alone. I do not want people watching me choose toilet paper in a supermarket or underwear in a department store. I don't like being alone, and I don't like the fact that I don't like being alone. Who in hell do I think I am? Is this what being a celebrity means? Am I becoming egotistical?

Somewhere along the road to celebrity status, I stopped sleeping in regular hotel rooms. It didn't happen overnight. Gradually, I realized that I was always staying in suites, with two separate rooms (sometimes three), step-up bathtubs (lit with recessed lights attached to a rheostat), an outer parlor, two bathrooms and two closets. On the table in front of the fake fireplace there is usually a basket of fruit covered with cellophane, and a champagne bottle with two glasses and a welcome note signed by the hotel's general manager. I like it.

Three years ago, on a trip to Las Vegas, I checked into the Las Vegas Hilton, and when the bellman opened my door and led the way into my room I was shocked to see that it was a plain, *regular* room! I was embarrassed by my feelings.

The bellman placed my one suitcase on the luggage stand, and I tipped him $5.

More recently, on a visit to the same hotel in Vegas, I approached the desk, was recognized and proudly stood by while the desk man searched for my room key. Because I am a celebrity, my reservation had been taken out of the routine system. Result: nobody could find my room key. I was standing at the desk and I was getting angry. Another attack of "celebrityitis?" Finally they found my key, apologized dramatically, and I was escorted upstairs. Imagine my relief when I walked into a full-blown suite complete with mirror over the bed. When the operator called to inquire if I wanted my calls "screened," I said, "Oh, would you? Thank you." Then I tore into the cellophane covering the fruit-and-cheese basket, pulled out an apple, sat down in a wing-backed French Provincial chair, took a huge bite and wondered what the hell was happening to me!

I find celebrity status difficult to bear when I am in the company of my mother. She'll say, "Oh, let's not go that way; Phil will be mobbed!" I am immediately concerned that if we do go that way I won't be mobbed and my mother will be disappointed. I also find that I am resentful of people who, when walking with me in public, will say, "Gee, you were hardly recognized by anybody." I am upset knowing that my companions are watching to see if I will be mobbed. If I am not mobbed they are disappointed, and I feel responsible. My celebrityhood is diminished for them, and I am bothered by the fact that I am bothered by that. Why should I care?

I am beginning to understand the special neuroses of famous people. I believe celebrity spoils people—some worse than others. I notice my tolerance level is dropping. I am impatient in lines—whether for taxis, airplane tickets, restaurant tables, license plates. I, the slow learner, am beginning to understand what being spoiled means, and I am determined to keep it under control.

Being a celebrity also has its countless subtle humiliations:

Two women meet me in a public place. "Oh, my goodness; it is really you. What in the world are you doing *here?* This is my sister; she doesn't know who you are." If I'm alone, I can handle this. If I'm with friends, I am embarrassed because my friends are embarrassed thinking that I am embarrassed by not being recognized—and it all happened right in front of them. I want to say to my friends, "Don't worry, this doesn't bother me; it happens all the time," but this will just prolong the agony, and I'm afraid that if I bring it up they'll think

I'm just being defensive and trying to cover up the fact that I'm embarrassed.

Even worse is the encounter with an old friend and *his* friend. The first says to the other, "Look who's here!" The other stares blankly. The first, embarrassed, exclaims, "You don't know who this is?" I stand helplessly. I am embarrassed for my friend who is embarrassed that *his* friend doesn't even know who I am. I don't care, but the friend does. Or do I?

Unless you're Sinatra or Hope or Carson, you are going to have to deal with a nagging feature of semistardom—the fan who can't think of your name. It happens to me all the time, and I am not sure why I resent it. I do not want to identify myself and resent being asked to, probably for two reasons: one, it is an invasion of privacy; and two, I am feeling the ego damage caused by a person who does not know who I am. I have definitely become hooked on celebrityhood, and when I think that that may not always be mine in a rapidly changing youth-worshiping culture made up of a very fickle public, I am feeling very anxious indeed.

Recently, at poolside in Miami Beach, as I lay on my back, well covered with Hawaiian Tropic suntan lotion . . . feeling very proud, wealthy and successful . . . a tall woman wearing very large sunglasses leaned over my sweaty body. Vacationers at a nearby bar were looking on.

"I hear you're a very famous person," she said. "Who are you?"

2
Beginnings

I AM Phillip John Donahue. I was born to Phillip and Catherine Donahue (née McClory) on December 21, 1935, at St. John's Hospital on Detroit Street in Cleveland, Ohio. Through my first eight years of life, I grew physically at about the same pace as America's climb out of The Great Depression.

In 1943 my parents bought their first house, 16108 Southland Avenue in Cleveland—brand-new, two-story, full basement, one bath, three bedrooms, $9,600. My sister, Kathy, was still a small baby, and I was a stalwart 7 years of age. The five-year separation between me and my sister amounted to light years . . . as children we functioned in separate universes. We never shared the same school or the same friends. It was much later, when we were both well into adulthood, that I came to really know my sister. Today we share a close and caring friendship.

The war wasn't over yet, but I had no doubt it would be soon, and of course there were no worries about who would win it. (The inevitability of America winning all the wars it entered was part of the national consciousness.)

I wore a small silver Liberty Bell replica that hung from a small golden banner which read REMEMBER PEARL HARBOR and boasted about my Uncle Jim (my mother's brother) who was in the Battle of the Bulge, was wounded and was held prisoner before finally being liberated by the Allies at the end of the war. I remember Roosevelt's death and how impressed I was by that historic event—not because I understood F.D.R.'s place in history, but because my favorite radio program, *Tom Mix*, cancelled its regular episode and played melancholy music, including the late President's favorite song, "Home on the Range."

My mother invented "conscientious." She never missed a meal or a bed change. If she were a man she might have run The Coca-Cola Company. She saw that my father always had clean socks and shirts and the other more important things he needed, like approval and someone who'd listen after he'd spent twelve hours on his feet selling furniture. Her life's energy was totally directed to our family, and however much gumption rested in the spirit of my dad, even he would admit that he was "nowhere without Catherine."

My dad was an air-raid warden during the war. He wore a white helmet, and while his duties were obscure, life was exciting during those practice raids when all the lights in the neighborhood (the world?) were turned out so that the "enemy" could not spot our cities from the air. I also remember ration coupons, fashioning huge balls of tinfoil, victory gardens, scarce nylon stockings and blue- and gold-star banners hanging in the windows of the homes of "our boys overseas."

When it all ended, the family drove to Kamm's Corners (our nearest commercial shopping area) and while my dad honked the horn jubilantly I stretched my arm out the window and formed the "V-for-Victory" sign. Later, as the student body of Our Lady of the Angels (O.L.A.) School stood at the curb on Rocky River Drive, a large caravan passed by led by an open convertible. Seated proudly on the top of the back seat, military cap in place, was General of the Army Dwight D. Eisenhower, waving at a sea of small American flags held by thousands of adults and children. High school bands added to the grandeur of the event.

At train stations all over America the "boys" were coming home, and while women kissed them till their hats fell off and the bands played and the confetti flew, it seemed the whole country was running on pride. We were proud we had won, proud we had defeated not only the Germans but the "Japs" as well. (How we used to scream at the Saturday-afternoon movie when the funny-looking "Jap" pilot cried out in panicky Japanese as his plane's canopy filled up with holes and blood appeared at his mouth, and then the cut to actual footage of the Zero spinning wildly out of the sky and crashing into the ocean with a big splash. More screams of approval from the audience of future soldiers.) We were proud to be Americans and proud that we weren't like those "Japs," who had "no respect for life" and who actually flew kamikaze planes into our battleships. "Japs" were sneaky and we were proud to defeat them. Proud we weren't like them.

If the seeds of racism and chauvinism were not sown they were certainly nurtured inside Cleveland's Riverside Theater on Lorain Street on Saturday afternoons. Today we can only speculate how much of that prejudice was left over in the hearts and minds of countless young people who sat through those two-reelers waiting for America to punch the "Japs" in the nose and who later supported America's Vietnam war effort right down to the last plastic zipper bag. Years later when General William Westmoreland told a television interviewer that the North Vietnamese "don't have any respect for life," I thought about how much we cheered during those movies and how small the jump is from "Japs" to "gooks."

Much later I would wonder about the whole phenomenon of pride—and how central a part it plays in all of man's conflicts. What is pride? Why does it manifest itself so, over man-made imaginary boundaries? Why, for example, if I had nothing to say about it, am I so proud to be Irish? And why has this feature of the human psyche remained so largely unexamined by behaviorists? Are pride and goose pimples and martial music good for us? Perhaps, as one sage put it, we suffer not from a lack of love, but from too much devotion.

Imagine my pride when, after the war, Bob Feller returned to the pitching mound for the Cleveland Indians and threw a no-hitter at the almighty Yankees. Then, as if we hadn't enough to be proud of, the Indians, behind their boy manager/shortstop Lou Boudreau, won the pennant and the World Series in 1948. The event was so extraordinary that the nuns allowed us to listen to the World Series games on radio—right in the classroom of Our Lady of the Angels, and right in the middle of the school day. Unprecedented. Boy, was I proud.

One entire wall of my bedroom was covered with portrait photos of every member of the Cleveland Indians, including the trainer. For more than a little while I went to bed every night being stared at by the likes of Bob Lemon, Kenny Keltner, Joe Gordon, Lou Boudreau, Dale Mitchell, Steve Gromek, Bob Kennedy and a host of other men who performed in a real world the way I performed in fantasy. By then I had made the O.L.A. baseball team as a second baseman, and while I was a passable glove man, I was not, in the language of the kids at Pop's soda fountain after the game, able to "hit shit." I recall one whole season during which I hit safely only twice, and both hits were in the same game. But however substandard my hitting ability, there was one baseball talent I had mastered. At the end of an inning, I could throw my glove to the outfield grass just like Lou Boudreau.

Nevertheless, I was proud. Proud to be an American, a Clevelander (The Best Location in the Nation), and most of all proud to be Catholic, and better yet proud to be the best kind of Catholic, an Irish one.

Baseball was not the only after-school activity for Little Philly. (The Cleveland Irish had a tradition of placing two syllables in the first name of most males—whether they wanted them or not. Patty Cochran, Tommy Corrigan, Jimmy Stanton, Timmy McIntyre, Philly Donahue.) I also took—hang on to your tutu—tap-dancing lessons. For a while I was the only boy in the class at Joyce Manning's dance studio at 98th and Lorain on Cleveland's West Side. The class also included at least twenty minutes of basic ballet. My dad thought it would give me "confidence," and I thought it would help me play second base and "turn" the double play like Joe Gordon. I am amazed to this day that I was able to emotionally tolerate being the only boy in a class of preadolescent girls dutifully moving through the five basic ballet positions and winding up with a plié.

The Joyce Manning Dance Studio's annual recital was held at Cleveland's Music Hall. So at age ten, Little Philly, with only a little "confidence," walked out on that big stage, blinded by a huge spotlight, faced a chasm of darkness, waited for the music to begin and tapped his way nervously through an uneven rendition of

> Brush those tears from your eyes . . .
> And try to realize . . .
> That the ache in my heart is for you . . .

Meanwhile, back at Our Lady of the Angels School, George O'Donnell* was beating the hell out of me. He said I had pushed him down the stairs. In retaliation, he pinned me on the sidewalk alongside the Rocky River Drive. A bus stopped; the driver opened the passenger door and, with authority, ordered George off me. Why I pushed George O'Donnell, who was more than twice my size, is any analyst's guess. Several years later, he and I were to spend four years at Notre Dame as roommates, an experience made possible by that bus driver.

I am still not clear why I was so combative as a kid. It certainly wasn't because I was tough. I have successfully repressed most of the

---

* This West Cleveland Irishman escaped the two-syllable tradition. He weighed 150 pounds in grammar school, and no one would have dared call him "Georgie."

details, but I know that of the many fights I had, I lost most of them. Some were very traumatic, like the time Bobby Keats washed my face with snow. The experience quite literally took my breath away. For an eternal moment, I was certain my breath was not coming back. I will never forget the humiliation of being left in the snow with a chapped face, gasping for air and watching helplessly as a larger, overpowering adversary laughed and walked away. I was so mad I went to his home and complained to his dad. His father listened patiently, said he'd "check into it" and closed the front door. Today I realize that that father was probably proud that his son wasn't "a sissy." That experience is still a part of me and always will be. I think about how painful bullyism can be and how our macho culture promotes it. I also think of all those "Phillys" who every day get more than a snow job in the face, and I think of how wasteful is this energy and how painful are its effects. I honestly cannot remember what, if anything, I did to provoke Bobby Keats, and why he responded as he did, but I feel that somewhere in this one-to-one male encounter is a clue to why men go to war.

Today, I confess that I am still thinking about Bobby Keats and wondering what happened to him. I am ashamed to acknowledge that wherever he is and whatever he is doing, I hope he is miserable.

On another occasion, Phil Dorenkott and I agreed to meet at the corner of Southland and Rocky River Drive to square off following an exchange of angry words on Halloween night. At twelve o'clock, high noon, I showed up at the appointed vacant lot with my best friend, Tommy Mott (he was only half Irish, but we gave him two syllables anyway). So there were two Phils, going at each other, bare fists and all! (It is instructive that while I remember all my fights I cannot recall the reason for any of them.) Dorenkott and Donahue were swinging away, and—honestly—I was doing okay. He seemed to be backing up, and I was taking the offensive, when I suddenly came to—sitting on my butt, with Tommy Mott inquiring about my well-being. Emotionally, I survived the defeat. The pain and the damage to my pride were not so great that I couldn't shake the winner's hand, congratulate him for his victory and depart on my bicycle.

But on the way home Tommy Mott inflicted still more pain. He actually said to me, aloud (and this is a quote), "I had an idea that was gonna happen." I may not always remember yesterday's show guest, but I will never forget those back-to-back "K.O.s" on that day in Cleveland in the mid-forties.

My last fistfight was with "Binky" Birt. His parents ensured that he would have a nickname when they christened him Vincent. As usual, I have no idea why we were fighting. All I remember is his bloody nose and mine. Now, at age 43, I am curious about this behavior and have more than a passing interest in understanding it. Why Little Philly was continually walking into losing conflicts has to do with fear.

I believe I fought because I was scared. Fighting proved to others that I wasn't scared. The only way I could show the other guys that I wasn't scared was to fight. Apparently losing was better than having my fear exposed. The real dilemma with this strategy was that after I fought and lost, and possibly convinced others that I wasn't scared, I was left with the knowledge that I was still scared. I realize now that what's important is not what others think, but what I know. And believe me, I knew I was scared. It would have been so much easier just to accept being scared and forgo the bloody nose.

Why some boys are more interested than others in proving they are not scared is a more interesting (and more important) question.

The all-male St. Edward High School was founded in 1949, just in time for Philly, who did not have the scholarship to attend the more prestigious and more challenging Jesuit high school, St. Ignatius. About one hundred young West Cleveland boys were to form the first class. Our new building, complete with gym and residence area for the Brothers of Holy Cross, would not be completed until our junior year. That meant two years of high school in two old Victorian houses near the site of the proposed school. It also meant a sense of pioneering which gave this crowd of teen-agers a strong sense of brotherhood not possible in the huge superschools so common in America today. Since no class was ahead of us, this select group of young men was never obliged to look up to any other student—we were always "senior," and when we graduated we proudly claimed to be, in every way, the first in the school's history.

It meant four years of being "first" at everything. "First" football team, "first" band, "first" concert, "first" sophomores and so on. I joined the band and proudly blew into a clarinet during the "first" Christmas party. Our repertoire was limited to "Jingle Bells" and "Silent Night," but no one complained. I was also the "first" artist on the "first" edition of the school newspaper and played a small role in our "first" school play, titled *An American Living Room*. I took Zita Mullen to our "first" dance, but because my dad drove us to and from the affair I was not able to transact my "first" kiss during that memorable evening. (That was to come later, on Jane Halloran's front porch. I actually asked her permission. She sighed, as in resignation, and then with some impatience she closed her eyes, puckered her lips and then opened them only long enough to say, "Okay, but make it quick," whereupon we engaged in the briefest and driest moment in all erotica.)

By our third year we had moved into the beautiful new St. Edward High School building on Detroit Street in suburban Lakewood, Ohio. The band had moved beyond "Jingle Bells" and into John Philip Sousa and even the Grieg *Piano Concerto,* featuring soloist Danny Kane at the piano. I was falling in love with a new girl every week. I was quite fascinated by girls and usually dated the most popular ones about twice before being replaced by a football player or some guy with a D.A. haircut and his own car.

Saturday nights were usually spent at the St. Christopher Canteen. The girls wore angora sweaters and rolled-down bobby sox with penny loafers. They always carried oversize wallets containing photo portfolios an inch and a half thick. Guy Mitchell was hot then ("One of the Roving Kind," "My Heart Cries for You"). The Saturday-night dances were the best thing that ever happened to horny boys, because you could move in, dance close, then closer and then, if you got lucky, cheek to cheek—without saying anything. All you had to do was "sense" it. Each little move closer was as subtle as a glance in church, and a girl could just as subtly avoid the escalation. This meant you could "communicate" intentions without anyone else knowing and without even acknowledging the little drama to each other. When you got rejected, you and she were the only ones who knew. Sometimes you got real lucky and suddenly there you were dancing to "My Heart Cries for You," surrounded by the white spots of the revolving mirrored ball, and you could feel her breasts against your chest—and you knew right away whether she was wearing a stiff-wire-reinforced bra or a plain soft one. The plain ones gave me the most bad thoughts.

A "bad thought" was what you got in 1953 when you saw a girl on the bus wearing a tight sweater. It was also any of a lot of other erotic images conjured up by bored adolescent boys in geometry class, or any other class. "Bad thoughts" were very handy when you were required to go to confession with the rest of the school and you couldn't think of any "sins." Sometimes I had trouble remembering how many bad thoughts I had had since my last confession, but I worked out my own moral code on the matter, reasoning that if I came within ten of being accurate, God would bless my intentions and give me absolution anyway.

When the record ended, you were able to give one last little squeeze with your hand on her back, and when you finally parted, you noticed that your perspiration had stuck her flattened hair to the side of her forehead.

Donna Rae Brougham was one of my most intense heartthrobs. One eventful Easter, I bought her a corsage and we went for a ride in the afternoon in advance of the big dance at the Columbia Ballroom that evening. (Unlike the St. Christopher Canteen, Columbia was for adults and had real live music. After all, it was Easter and my date was the highly regarded Donna Rae.) During the drive she said she had something to tell me, but that she wanted to wait till that evening, "because if I tell you now you won't want to go out with me tonight." Naturally I stopped the car immediately and demanded the information "right now." You can imagine what was going through my mind. After much hesitation she haltingly said, "I'm joining the convent."

We went out that night anyway, and I remember it as one of the more depressing evenings of my social calendar. Here I was, trying to dance cheek to cheek with a girl who at the same time was one of the cutest coeds on the West Side, was wearing a soft bra and was joining the convent, for God's sake! My guilt was overwhelming! In my quest for girls' favor, I was accustomed to vying with quarterbacks, auto owners and guys with "duck's-ass" haircuts, but competing with Jesus was more than I could handle.

Notre Dame

IN 1953 there were two ways for an Irish Catholic boy to impress his parents, his neighbors and his girlfriend: become a priest or attend Notre Dame. When my letter of acceptance to N.D. arrived, I framed it and hung it on my bedroom wall, right where Bob Lemon used to be. In spite of my largely mediocre report card from St. Edward High School, the power brokers within the Holy Cross community of priests and brothers chose to accept all the first graduates from St. Ed's who expressed interest in Notre Dame. Both schools are operated by the Holy Cross religious community. I knew I was lucky then, and as the years pass, and the required S.A.T. scores get higher, and the tuition approaches $7,000 per year, I no longer think of it as luck—rather as divine intervention.

Arriving in South Bend, Indiana, with a suitcase and a metal box for mailing dirty laundry home, I moved into my abode for the coming year, 115 Zahm Hall. My dorm rector was Father Fryberger, who had the most sinister reputation of any of Notre Dame's residence-hall priest/policemen. Fryberger mythology included a report that he often ran down the hall late at night wearing one shoe—thus giving the impression he was walking, and enabling this supersleuth to catch frolicking freshmen in acts of disobedience.

The rules at Notre Dame were strict and simple in 1953. All students were to be in their dorms by 10 o'clock on weeknights and 12 midnight on weekends. To ensure an accurate inventory, football jocks made a visual room check in the evening, and post–10-o'clockers were obliged to sign in at the door under the suspicious eye of a campus policeman who wore a real badge. Students were also under orders to sign in on a centrally located dorm roster before 7 o'clock on three weekday mornings per week. This was to encourage attendance at Mass on at least these days. The Notre Dame administration reasoned correctly that the way to a young man's soul was through his alarm clock and that for many young men of Notre Dame the presence of the Holy Spirit might not be enough. Thus "morning check." Failure to sign in three times a week earned the delinquent student "dawn patrol," a Fryberger innovation that obliged the violator to sign in at 6 A.M. each day the following week.

Generally speaking, the system worked. Although a student could sign in and return to the comfort of his still-warm sack, weekday Masses in most hall chapels (each residence hall at Notre Dame has a chapel) were reassuringly crowded.

My roommate at Notre Dame was George O'Donnell, my sparring partner from Cleveland. Time had healed the emotional wounds I sustained on the sidewalk beside Rocky River Drive, and our plan to room together had been agreed upon before we went to South Bend. Beginning my first life expereince away from home in the daily company of George O'Donnell was to have a pervasive influence on me, and somewhere in my psyche I still feel the consequences of this four-year experience in a way I may never fully understand.

First, and most important, I perceived George as immensely more gifted than I in almost every way. George had gone to the Jesuit high school St. Ignatius, and I to the newly formed, less challenging school run by the Holy Cross Brothers. In the world of holy letters, when you saw the Holy Cross C.S.C. following the proper name of a priest or brother, you knew he was holy. When you saw the Jesuit S.J. after a name, you knew he was smart. It mattered not which was the better school or the "better" order of religious; what was important was that Catholic folklore had the Jesuits definitely in first place in Academe— Jesuits studied longer (more than twenty years before ordination), claimed the largest order of priests around the world and reported to a man who sat in Rome in the shadow of His Holiness himself, the Pope. (One local joke had three priests from different orders asking God which was His favorite. A note floated down reassuring the three that the Almighty looked with equal favor and love on all of them. The note was signed, *God, S.J.*)

George had graduated from St. Ignatius with honors and had distinguished himself not only in Latin but in Greek as well. I not only had barely graduated from the "less challenging" St. Ed's, but from the first freshman "language option" was shuffled off to French and away from the more demanding Latin. The unspoken axiom had the smart kids in Latin, the dumb kids in French. George could conjugate verbs aloud—in Latin—much to the amazement of the first-floor community in Zahm Hall, and much to the dismay of "Little Philly," who was still wondering how he had got there and scared to death that he wasn't going to survive at "Our Lady's University."

George and I had played together on the Our Lady of Angels baseball team, where he had hit home runs and I had hung in for bases on balls. Even our positions conveyed my sense of social placement vis-à-vis George. He played First; I played Second.

If my third-grade fight with George at O.L.A. was provoked by hidden admiration and fear of him, then so was much of what I did at Notre Dame in that memorable freshman year. When George returned his uniform to the ROTC with the simple announcement that he "didn't care to be in the Army," I did the same thing. When George went to the movies, I went to the movies, and he usually chose which one. When George signed up for interhall football, I signed up. It didn't matter that I had never played organized football in my life. There I was, at the home of the Fighting Irish, actually studying mimeographed play sheets with X's and O's.

In our first game I was hit so hard from behind while running a pass pattern that I do not remember the second half, the walk back to the dorm, the shower, the walk to the "caf" for dinner or the dinner itself. I "woke up" returning from supper—groggy and confused. After I went to bed early that night, George, who had a maddening interest in practical jokes, reset my alarm, turned out the lights and then gathered the first-floor gang to await the pandemonium. A few minutes later the alarm went off; I jumped out of bed, quickly dressed and was running down the hall for Morning Mass Check when I heard the laughter. "Good Ol' George" had done it again. The time was 7 P.M., not 7 A.M. Under my breath I said, "You son of a bitch," and slowly made my way back to room 115.

However intimidating my relationship with "Good Ol' George," as he came to be known, it had many positive features. My admiration for his intelligence and his popularity never flagged, and we shared many laughs during that year and the three that followed. A small clique of freshmen whom we called "The Gang" had formed around George. His gregarious, cavalier nature was very attractive to the other law-and-order guys who, like me, were very much focused on obeying the rules and getting safely through that uncharted freshman year.

I had been a student at Notre Dame only two months when a registered letter arrived in my mailbox which was to age me two years in the next two weeks. The letter was on the stationery of St. Ignatius High School (George's school) and was postmarked Cleveland, Ohio.

Dear Phillip,
Mary* has told me the whole story. My wish is to have you both reconciled to the Church. I know this is a difficult matter for you both, but I am confident that with God's help we can resolve this problem.

Since you were married outside the Church, it will be necessary either for the marriage to be annulled or for you both to receive God's forgiveness in the Sacrament of Penance and reestablish your union with God's grace within Holy Matrimony.

It is important that I speak with you at once. Kindly contact me as soon as possible.

Meanwhile, I remain ever devoted in Christ,
                                                        A. V. Kanuch, S.J.

I read the letter and immediately concluded that this was George O'Donnell's idea of a joke and said under my breath, "You son of a bitch."

"I swear I did not write that letter," George said.

"Baloney," I said.

"Honest to God," he said.

I sat down and wrote a letter to Father Kanuch in an attempt to call George's bluff. I said that not only was I not married, I had no idea who Mary was. Further, it was "clear to me that someone is playing a joke."

Three days later another registered letter arrived from Father Kanuch assuring me that "this is no joke. Please contact me so that I may begin the serious business of reconciling you and Mary to Holy Mother Church."

Now two things were happening: I was suffering from near-terminal anxiety and the first floor of Zahm Hall was alive with speculation about "the broad Donahue knocked up and has to marry."

I took my dilemma to Father Thomas Baker, a short, likable young

* A fictitious name.

priest who was the freshman chaplain, residing in Kavanaugh Hall, another freshman dorm. I gave him both letters and swore that I was not married, never had been and was not given to amnesia or weekend drunkenness. He asked if I minded if he shared this problem with another, more experienced priest, in confidence. I said no, and we arranged to meet the following night. (Back in Zahm Hall, the freshman men of Notre Dame were asking "D'ja hear about Donahue?" and George was holding hall news conferences for exam-weary freshmen who were starved for scandal.)

The following night I showed up at Father Baker's office with my high school yearbook in hand. I bounded into the room and volunteered that I had hit on a great idea which would end all the confusion. I would send various pictures of my high school classmates, including one of me, and Father Kanuch could challenge Mary to pick mine. I was convinced that Mary had spent a long weekend with someone who had given her my name to avoid later hassles. I was also convinced that she had just discovered she was pregnant and was on a vigorous search for "Phil Donahue."

Father Baker thought about the idea and then said, haltingly, that he did not want me to be offended by the question he was about to ask, but that it nevertheless should be asked. "Is there," he asked awkwardly, "possibly any other woman you might have been with recently who, after intimacy and a possible pregnancy, might have given Father Kanuch the false name of Mary?"

"Father, I swear to you," I answered, "I have never been to bed with a girl. I do not know this woman and I know of no girl who would be capable of telling this kind of lie to a priest. Please believe me."

We agreed that the high school photos should be sent to Father Kanuch and that my folks should be notified.

Immediately after the briefing, my mother called Father Kanuch to say, "My son has been going to Communion. I know he wouldn't do that if he had this matter on his conscience." Catholics in a state of mortal sin, which mine definitely would have been, are forbidden to receive Holy Communion without a pardon in the confessional. However plausible my alleged "sin," my mother was convinced that I would not have committed the sacrilege of accepting the Holy Eucharist while not in the state of grace.

Unfortunately, she was my mother, and her testimony was taken as it would have been in a court of law—with a grain of salt. I can hear Father Kanuch now, saying to my mother in a patronizing way that only another Jesuit could match, "Yes, Mrs. Donahue. There, there, everything will be all right."

Three days later I received a phone call from Father Kanuch. It was my first oral communication with him. I walked into the phone booth on the first floor of Zahm Hall next to the mailboxes. I closed the door and, as always in a tense situation, I began to talk.

"Father, obviously what's happened here is some guy who knows me got this girl pregnant and—"

A thin, aging voice at the other end of the phone said, "Phillip, she's not pregnant."

I was thrown by the declaration and also by the cold, monklike formality of the delivery—his use of my full name, Phillip. Recovering, I continued, "Well, whether she's pregnant or not, Father, I am convinced that somebody spent a weekend with this young woman and gave her my name to avoid future complications. I do not know this girl and I know she doesn't know me."

After a slight pause the voice on the phone, almost inaudible, said, "Yes, Phillip, but she identified your picture."

My head flushed and a ringing began in my ears and sweat appeared on my forehead and on the palms of my hands. I began to cry. Somebody was trying to really screw me, and I didn't know who or why. "I'm coming to Cleveland," I said.

"Now, Phillip, that isn't necessary . . ."

"I'm coming to Cleveland now."

"Phillip, be sensible . . ."

"You can't stop me!"

"Phillip, your studies . . ."

"I'm coming to Cleveland."

I hung up the phone, blew my nose and called United Airlines for a reservation on what was to be my first flight ever, anywhere.

That night I went to the Grotto alone. Notre Dame's Grotto is second only to Sacred Heart Church in terms of holy real estate on campus. It is a beautiful, quiet spot behind Corby Hall, home of Notre Dame's resident priests, and very near St. Joseph's Lake. The seasons are no more beautifully manifest than at the Grotto of Our Lady at the fabled University of Notre Dame.

I made my way down the steps and moved past the iron guardrail in front of the high stone wall that surrounds the statue of the Virgin. And there, in an alcove under the statue, I did something that I had seen my mother, my grandmother and my Aunt Ann do repeatedly throughout my childhood. I lit a candle.

I stood silently and alone, asking the Blessed Mother to keep me from panic and to make this nightmare end. The brittle South Bend November wind came in off St. Joseph's Lake and swept through the trees, shaking the last leaves of fall and flickering scores of candles whose light glanced off the stone. Then, ending my prayer, I silently retreated, as thousands of others had done before me.

When I arrived back at 115 Zahm Hall, George and three other members of The Gang were playing euchre. After donning my pajamas and brushing my teeth I climbed into bed, and as I punched a hole in my pillow I could hear the cards being slapped down on a flat suitcase while George absent-mindedly conjugated the verb "to love" in Latin: "*Amo, amas, amat, amamus, amantis, amant. . . .*" Under my covers and under my breath I heard myself say, "You son of a bitch."

After my maiden flight to Cleveland, during which I never took my eyes off the ground, I arrived at St. Ignatius High School and Father Kanuch met me at the front door, escorted me into a small anteroom and nervously said, "She's confessed." He went on to explain that my mother was waiting for me in another room and that I need worry no more. His face was drained. He looked like a stooped-over Jacques Cousteau. It was obvious that Father Kanuch, however long and faithful his service to God, had never before been through anything like this.

In that brief meeting with Father, I learned that a Mary Johnson had gone to him to "confess" that she had secretly married Phil Donahue outside the Church during a weekend visit to Kentucky. She had said, I was told, that she felt guilty and wanted to return to God and the Church. I also learned that Mary Johnson had seen me only once in her life—in that play at St. Edward High School titled *An American Living Room*. She had started to tell the truth when she was told I was en route to Cleveland for a confrontation. Father told me to wait in the hallway; Mary wanted to apologize to me.

The main hallway at St. Ignatius High School in Cleveland is dark and cathedral-like. Large framed pictures of the school's many graduating classes line the walls, their even rows of ovals exposing the faces of the thousands of young Catholic men who have attended West Cleveland's most prestigious Catholic boys' high school in search of knowledge and actual grace as only the "Jebbies" can impart it. Muted rays of light came in through the window above the door and refracted off the worn marble floor.

The footsteps down the hall were soft, but still set off a small echo.

I stood firmly, consciously forcing my face into what I felt was a stern expression, and as the footsteps moved closer my heart beat faster.

She stopped directly in front of me, and the light from above the door revealed a very plain young woman of 18 years with a plump, unattractive body. "I want you to know," she said quietly and with apparent sincerity, "I'm very sorry."

I looked at her for what felt like a long time. "Do you realize the anguish you have caused my family?"

"I'm really sorry," she said. We waited alone, surrounded by the eerie emptiness of a place built to accommodate large numbers of people. Its vastness made it appear more empty. More quiet. More strange. "You know"—and she then paused again.

"You know, what?" I asked.

She looked right at me and after a moment said, "You know, I think I'm crazy."

A year later, local newspapers reported that Cleveland police had questioned a woman claiming to have seen Dr. Sam Sheppard's wife murdered on the beach behind their Bay Village home. They discounted her story and told reporters she was a mental case. Police disclosed the woman's name as Mary Johnson.

Back at Notre Dame after the excitement of my first plane ride and the calm after the "Mary storm," I settled in for studies, exams, off-campus pizza and football weekends complete with loudspeakers which filled the campus with the "Notre Dame Victory March" and out-of-town girls who filled angora sweaters. Nowhere was the deficiency of unisex education more apparent than in Zahm Hall on football weekends. The "men" of Notre Dame were reduced to *Animal House* characters by the presence of young women who, it must be said, never prepared more conscientiously than when visiting South Bend for the big game. They were all beautiful, right down to the pompon with the blue-and-gold ribbon. Living all week with George O'Donnell and being constantly surrounded by male students at The Huddle coffee shop and in Cost Accounting class—everywhere—did more for weekend lust than any low-budget porn film.

The all-male school also retarded maturation. Although sexism was largely unexamined in the fifties, it was undoubtedly strengthened by that system which featured an all-male campus during the week and then, as in some wild and undisciplined experiment, introduced hundreds of beautiful women on football weekends. It also caused a lot of early marriages which were entered into for the wrong breathless reasons.

By spring of my freshman year it had become apparent that I could indeed meet the academic challenge of Notre Dame. But the challenge of surviving the suspicious review of Father Fryberger was quite another matter. Several incidents, including walking on the grass, making loud noise at night and planting a phony note in Louie Marks's mailbox informing him that he was "campused" for a weekend, brought both George and me to the brink of expulsion.

On one occasion we were ordered to appear separately before Father McCarragher, who had the ominous nickname "Black Mac," the Prefect of Discipline. I arrived at his office in the century-old main administration building at the appointed hour and waited prayerfully to be escorted inside. When I entered, Father McCarragher sat at his desk reviewing material which I assumed detailed all my substandard behavior, which was most certainly well documented by Father Fryberger, who had previously expressed his "wonder" to me. "Wonder about what, Father?" I had asked. "Wonder about whether you are University material," he had answered with a routinely raised eyebrow which made me feel he had delivered the same line under the same circumstances on thousands of other occasions.

I was motioned to be seated by Father McCarragher, who wanted an explanation for this series of misbehaviors.

"I believe it's immaturity, Father," I said humbly and with dramatic sincerity.

"Black Mac," with the certainty of a man who has been in this play for several seasons, suggested that "there's a reason for immaturity," and went on to tell me in no uncertain terms that I was the cause of the immaturity and that immaturity was no excuse and that I had better get my act together. I assured him that I was University material and was going to definitely change my ways and definitely improve my behavior and that I was definitely going to become an entirely different person so that I might take full advantage of the wonderful opportunities offered by the University of Notre Dame. Definitely.

Finally he raised his head, exposing a bright red Irish face that reminded me of all my uncles, and, peering at me from across a large mahogany desk and from behind wire-rimmed glasses, he delivered a line that had all the polish of years of practice: "I want you back here in two weeks, at which time we'll make a decision." He waited gravely for a response.

"A decision with regard to what, Father?" I asked, not surprisingly.

(With relish) "A decision with regard to whether or not you will remain at this University," he said.

The summer after my first year at Notre Dame I worked as a mason's helper at the Republic Steel mill in Canton, Ohio. (My dad had left the Bing Furniture Company in downtown Cleveland after many years of loyal service to go to work for a smaller company and larger pay in Canton.) A mason's helper accompanies the brickmason inside the open-hearth and blast furnaces during the regular shutdown time for relining. My job was to ensure that the mason always had a supply of bricks. The money was good, and when the furnace had recently been shut down, we received extra pay for "hot work." On some jobs the temperature exceeded 130 degrees. The union contract said "three minutes and out." It was so hot you couldn't sweat. I recall the discomfort of my blue jeans touching the skin of my leg. We all wore work shoes with steel-reinforced toes and, of course, the obligatory helmet.

For me, the job in the steel mill that summer was like aversion therapy. It made me more concerned about completing my college education and avoiding a lifetime blue-collar fate.

The Republic Steel mill in Canton was also a brand-new kind of school for me. It was my first exposure to the earthy language and traditions of the Appalachian white men who came north to find work and found it at more than $3 an hour thanks to God and the United Steelworkers of America.

They were burly men with bad teeth and large bellies, and for the most part, they ignored me. The chatter around the locker room and at the lunch break was vulgar and irreverent ("son of a bitch" had only two syllables) and spoke to issues like sex in a way I had never known before.

"If a woman wants it, she'll come up for it."

"Goddamn right."

"Fuckin'-A right."

"Sum bitch."

I spent weeks thinking about this, unable to tell anyone that this soon-to-be-sophomore at the University of Notre Dame actually wasn't sure what "come up for it" meant.

I remember the red faces of the men who threw coal into the open hearths and still wonder how badly their bodies were damaged by the strain and the temperature and the noise and all the crud in the air. I also remember the rats. Steel mills are filled with rats. They are initially attracted by the orange peels and other debris discarded by the men after their lunch break; then the rats find the heat of the steel mill to their liking. Steel mills are a rat's man-made paradise. Rats in steel mills don't walk or run; they waddle.

During one memorable lunch, I hurried through my sandwich to get to my Hostess Twinkies. (The sandwich was always ruined by the heat of the nearby furnaces. The butter melted through the bread, making it greasy and moist and barely edible. Usually, however, it was the only sandwich available, and it was better than being hungry.) I was about to bite into the first Twinkie—my sandwich chaser—when the heavyweight champion rat of the world waddled toward me, suddenly panicked, bumped into the steel-reinforced toe of my shoe and scrambled back under the nearest open hearth.

It was the first time in my life that I failed to finish a Hostess Twinkie.

In September I returned with relief to the sublimely beautiful campus of Notre Dame and to classes in Newtonian Physics, Cost Accounting, Calculus, Marketing and, last and most appealing to me, Philosophy and Theology. By then I had come to realize that I could handle Notre Dame; that I wasn't, after all, so damn dumb. Not as smart as George, but not dumb.

Our required Theology course included a review of books on the Index. This was a list of authors condemned by Holy Mother Church because of heresy or other material not consistent with Catholic teaching. Catholics were ordinarily forbidden to read them, but the theory at the time was that it was acceptable to expose the young men of Notre Dame to the contaminated literature as long as they were closely supervised by approved Catholic theologians. I loved it.

For other reasons as well, I was fascinated by Theology/Philosophy (at Notre Dame there was very little distinction between them) and even brought my enthusiasm for the subject into my social life. Somewhere in my first conversation with a new girlfriend I recall casually revealing that I was "just about finished with *Prolegomena to Any Future Metaphysic* by Immanuel Kant." God, was she impressed.

My Theology teacher was Father James Smyth, and I admired him more than any of my other teachers. I also got my best grades from him. An A+ on a paper explaining the Trinity.

> The Blessed Trinity is Three Persons in one Nature, not
> Three Persons in one Person. The Trinity is not a mathe-

matical contradiction. Person is Who one is, Nature is what something is. The Three Persons are all separate but equal in their Person, yet they . . . together . . . make up One Nature . . . God.

God the Father (the first Person) so loved the world, He sent His Only Begotten Son to earth to redeem us from our sins. On earth Jesus assumed a human nature, but remained essentially, Divine (the second Person). God the Father's love is expressed in the Holy Spirit (the third Person).

Imagine my horror when several years later, right on my stage, the Episcopal bishop James Pike was to refer to the Blessed Trinity as "excess baggage"! It was only one of many assaults on dogmatic Catholic theology that were to turn my head after my graduation from Notre Dame and Father Smyth's Theology course.

Nevertheless, that teacher and those courses were to enlarge me more than any other single academic experience. Father Smyth turned my "wonder wheels"—opened my mind to the possibility that beyond the questions and the memorized answers of the Baltimore Catechism there were untold areas of inquiry. Uncharted and sometimes scary areas. But they were there, and they could be examined not so much for answers as for the excitement of trying to discover them. When the body of Father Smyth was discovered in his room at Corby Hall, he had been dead eighteen hours (a heart attack). Does he now know the answers he so effectively encouraged his students to seek? I hope he does. I *wonder* if he does.

In Morrisey Hall (a sophomore dorm), George and I settled in for another year at Our Lady's University. Our new rector, Father Glen Boarman, told us that he didn't care about our past; he was concerned only about our future. He knew we were "Notre Dame material" and invited us to come see him anytime we needed help. He even taught me how to serve Mass, which I did, three or four times a week.

Gone were the Fryberger investigations, the "dawn patrols," the fear of being dismissed from Notre Dame. For the first time in my life, I was beginning to feel comfortable with myself. I was actually doing well in school (even Calculus), and George and I both became active in University Theatre. We were becoming a part of another community on campus, and the roles we won in major productions were meaty and challenging. (Our thespian life at Notre Dame came to an end in our senior year with our biggest triumph. George played Willy

Loman and I played Biff in *Death of a Salesman,* sensitively directed by Father Arthur Harvey.)

One of the new friends who came into my life by virtue of theater was a tall, thin, pipe-smoking chap by the name of Jim Cooney. Cooney had a great sense of humor, kept up with anybody's beer drinking and, most important of all, was mad about history. History was as close to death as I came at Notre Dame, with the exception of Black Mac; somehow History and I did not marry well. But Cooney kept me alive with intense twenty-minute briefings backstage during rehearsals.

Jim Cooney also introduced me to his sister, a Marquette freshman named Margie. Margie Cooney was a tall, attractive girl who looked sexy in an overcoat buttoned up around her neck. We dated during my junior year, but our courtship really began in earnest when, during my senior year, she quit school, moved in with her aunt in Chicago and got a job with Price Waterhouse in the Prudential Building in the Loop.

During the summer between my junior and senior years, I had worked hard at WNDU-TV, "the Notre Dame station"—NBC Television for South Bend, Indiana, and I kept the job (at one cool dollar an hour) through my last two semesters at N.D. This meant I had money, and with her receptionist job at Price Waterhouse she had money. Throw in the South Shore Line which runs between South Bend and Chicago and you've got a pretty romantic fantasy. Her aunt threw in a '51 Chevy and I thought I'd died and gone to heaven. We visited every bar in the Loop, had small talk across candles and wineglasses in rathskellers on the North Side and then sat, literally, all night long in the front seat of that Chevy. On more than one morning we saw the sun come up on North Janssen Avenue, happy but weary from fighting off mortal sin throughout the entire evening and through the long early morning hours.

At 6 A.M. we would roll down the windows to evaporate the steam on the windshield, and then I would walk her to her door, somewhat disheveled and more than somewhat in agony from unfulfilled passion. There would follow a long, amorous good-by, more agony and then the long walk to the Ravenswood El for the ride into the Loop and then to the South Shore for the longer ride back to South Bend. All the time I wondered how long I could realistically expect to remain monklike, when I was having so many bad thoughts.

4

Early Dayton

MY SENIOR year at Notre Dame was filled with classes, University Theatre and WNDU-TV. Although I was a business major, the television experience was beginning to occupy much of my time and enthusiasm. I had been hired as a set-up person, but it wasn't long before I moved into the microphone booth, filling in for an announcer who failed to make it in time for a station break. It is hard to describe what happens in your body the first time the large studio door closes on you, the red ON AIR light blitzes your eyes and the entire booth echoes with an awesome and intimidating silence that you have to fill. Hello, America! I remember *feeling* the perspiration appear on my forehead as I clutched my ear (thinking it would make my voice sound deeper) and said, in as august a tone as has ever been heard in the history of broadcasting, "This is the Notre Dame station, WNDU-TV, Channel Forty-six, South Bend." I did, honest to God, *hear* my heart beat. I was too scared to know it then, but I realize now that from that moment on, I was hooked.

Soon I was a regular announcer. I wasn't much good, but what else was available at a dollar an hour? I signed the station on every morning at 6:30 and sat through the entire *Today* show, reading station breaks, commercials over slides. (And all before Father Smyth's 9 A.M. Theology class!) Afternoons I did cutaways for the White Sox on radio —"At the end of three and a half, it's Sox five, Indians three."

During Easter vacation of my senior year I auditioned at KYW-TV in Cleveland and was hired as a summer replacement announcer.

Score a big one! George recalls me standing in front of the mirror above our sink saying: "This is Phil Donahue for Channel Three in Cleveland . . ." My dad and mom and all my old girlfriends would hear me. The day after graduation I walked first to St. John's Cathedral at 9th and Superior in downtown Cleveland, knelt down, said a prayer, lit a candle, then walked across the street to Channel 3, cleared my throat and welcomed myself to a job, to freedom from classes and to manhood.

God was being very good to me, but there was one thorn in Paradise Valley. Toward the end of my days at WNDU I had begun to suspect that announcing wasn't the most challenging job in broadcasting. Three weeks at KYW in Cleveland and I was sure of it. Sitting in a booth for 59 minutes and 30 seconds waiting to say, "Tom Field reports the news at eleven on KYW-TV, Channel Three, Cleveland . . . it's eight o'clock" not only was not great, it was very, very boring.

My father had sold his bass fiddle during the Depression so that he could eat. His show-business career had ended early for a very good reason: survival. Although he never said so, I always had the feeling that he was less than impressed with entertainers, and that his son the graduate of Notre Dame had not been given God's greatest education for selling Bosco in the kiddie cartoons. So it went without saying that I was expected to do more with my life than sit in a soundproof booth doing station breaks and marveling at my own resonance. In fact, a station owner in Albuquerque, a big Notre Dame supporter, later refused to hire me for just that reason—a graduate of Our Lady's University had no business in show business. I was vaguely uncomfortable with the idea, but I honestly think my greatest ambition at graduation had been to be a good announcer.

And I was in love. But Margie had gone home to her family in the Southwest. Loving pure and chaste at Notre Dame had been hard enough, but loving "pure and chaste from afar" was hell. We wrote to each other every day.

My dearest Margie, I'm sitting here (in a soundproof booth) watching the Steve Allen Show, *waiting to do a station break at 9 o'clock, and I'm thinking of you . . .* Her letters often spoke of an anxiety she had about people in television. Television attracts such self-centered people, she'd write. It could turn a normal man into an egomaniac who cared more about himself than his family, she'd worry. I kept assuring her I knew what she meant, but "that definitely won't happen to me."

By the time October 1957 rolled around, I was ready. I had audition tapes, films of me doing commercials and reading the news, and a very flattering reference letter from my summer boss in Cleveland. More important, I had an airplane ticket. I was off to meet my love, find a job in television in a new and exciting city, and get married. I arrived in Albuquerque on Friday. On the following Friday I still had no job in television. One station program director said I had an accent. The others didn't say much of anything. I was in shock. Here I was, a graduate of Notre Dame, with experience in the tenth-largest market in the country, and no one in what I began to think of as "this goddamn desert town" of Albuquerque would hire me.

I checked the classifieds and found what sounded like a very attractive job opportunity. Something about being in business for yourself and making as much as $20,000 a year. At the instructed time and place I was there, best suit, shoes shined. When the man stood up with a set of knives, a wooden holder that attaches to the kitchen wall and the line "There are three hundred thousand people in this town and they're waiting for you to sell them," I almost passed out from embarrassment. My parents had just put me through four years at one of America's most expensive universities, and less than a year later I was within an inch of selling knives door to door. Suddenly booth announcing looked like an IBM vice-presidency. Six days later I began sorting checks in the transit department of the Albuquerque National Bank. It wasn't CBS, but at least I could write home and tell the truth.

On February 1, 1958, in one of the oldest Catholic churches in America, San Felipe de Neri, in the Old Town section of Albuquerque, New Mexico, in a Solemn High Nuptial Mass (three priests), Phillip John Donahue and Margaret Mary Cooney were "joined together" in matrimony.

Two months later I sent a letter to my former boss at KYW in Cleveland saying, "Have wife, will travel." In June of 1958 in a '57 Chevy Bel Air (white with red interior) filled with everything we owned, we drove into Cleveland for Round Two of summer announcing. We found an "apartment" on West Boulevard (more accurately described as an attic in the house of a retired Cleveland policeman. He had furnished the place himself, right down to the silverware). It wasn't *House Beautiful*, but for the newlyweds from Albuquerque, it was perfect.

There was only one problem. We had been married in February, and it was already June and we still weren't pregnant. I was convinced I was sterile. In September I got the good news and the bad news. The good news was we were going to have a baby. The bad news was we couldn't afford it. The vacation schedule had ended at KYW, and I had had absolutely no success in landing a job at any other station in Cleveland. I auditioned everywhere—WHK, WGAR, WJW, WEWS . . . nothing! Now I had a pregnant wife, and as I couldn't find a broadcasting job anywhere else, I wound up counting money in the basement of the National City Bank in Cleveland, waiting to be "promoted" to the transit department, where I could sort checks again.

After about two weeks of playing Bob Cratchit, I got a phone call and what was probably the biggest break I've ever had in my career. It was Bernie Barth, my general manager from WNDU in South Bend, with a tip on a radio job in Adrian, Michigan, at 250-watt WABJ. A 250-watter is the smallest they come. You can't broadcast at less than 250 watts on a commercial frequency. But I was euphoric. I was back in broadcasting, and I wasn't sterile.

My title was Program/News Director. My pay was $500 per month. My staff consisted of five very young D.J.s. And for the first time I was doing something more than "rip and read"—pulling wire copy off the AP machine and enunciating clearly. I was out chasing stories. I covered City Hall. I covered my first murder and my first fatal auto accident and got sick when the ambulance driver poked at the victim's neck for a pulse.

It was also my first close look at a member of the community of men who make up what I suppose we will forever call "management." In Adrian, Michigan, "management" was one overweight millionaire. He happened to own the station. James Gerrity was famous for calling the nighttime disc jockey and demanding, "Give me more brass; I want brass!" Brass was all we'd play for the next three weeks. Once he assigned me to check the license plates of all cars parked in front of the Bridgeport Brass Company, a firm he had once owned and suspected was being sold. My mission (and I had no choice but to accept it) was to find out who the buyers were going to be. For Christmas, James Gerrity gave his employees a silver-plated candle snuffer and a book titled *Wisdom*. Just what expectant newlyweds needed.

It was inevitable I'd have a great First Amendment experience. In the news business it's like losing your virginity. It happened to me in an ice cream factory. One day I stopped by the local dairy to ask the man who owned it some questions. I don't even remember the story, only that he was an Adrian city commissioner and that I had every right to make the inquiry. He apparently thought they were the wrong questions, because he threw me out. With that rather undignified experience came my first realization of the potentially explosive power of journalism. Even in small-town journalism, it's not so much the nature of the material you are dealing with as the nature of the egos involved.

For the first time I was beginning to question the people I'd always looked up to, the people who had succeeded—those who owned their own businesses, the judges, the mayor, members of the city council, all the examples of the Puritan ethic. And I was quite suddenly in a position to see the power structure up close, at an equal level. I saw a tight little network of insecure, egocentric men who knew how truly vulnerable they were, and as a result tried like hell to manipulate the reporters who wrote about them. I was rapidly learning that the image I'd grown up with—wise and virtuous men in gray three-piece suits—was not consistent with reality. It wasn't a stunning instant recognition. It came in little bits and pieces—like the great police scandal. Among the town cops there not only were no sharpshooters: some of those deadeyes couldn't even hit the target. I didn't create the scandal, I just reported it, but in doing so I became an important player in the drama.

I covered a strike in a nearby town called Tecumseh, at a little factory where they made one- and two-stroke engines. I talked with the union. I talked with the management. And when the strike was over I called the vice-president of industrial relations for a comment about the settlement. He didn't know what to say.

"Well, say the terms of the settlement were mutually beneficial to all parties."

"What was that?" he said.

"Mutually beneficial to all parties," I said.

I went on the air that night and quoted the V.P.: "The terms are mutually beneficial to all parties." I don't know why that did it for me, but it was the beginning of the realization that the fact that a man is vice-president doesn't necessarily mean he's smart. The crown of the big-shot gray-vested businessman, whom I had looked up to as a child, was beginning to slip.

This, as they say on the newscast, was an "important development," because a child in the fifties absolutely did not question the establishment. There just wasn't much rebellion going on. The most horrendous thing I ever did was soap windows on Halloween, not question authority. But at age 23, not only was I in a position to make the establishment respond to my questions, I had a faintly perceived sense of my responsibility to ask loaded ones and the "fat cats'" responsibility to answer them. My access and ability to force answers didn't come from any sort of financial equality. I wasn't making big money. I wasn't anybody. My power was the fact that I would quote them on the radio. I was responsible for delivering their thoughts to the 23,000 people of Adrian, Michigan. Within broadcasting I had discovered this terribly exciting cerebral pursuit which was satisfying and adventuresome—and it had power. I was a news reporter, and by God, don't let any Albuquerque general manager tell me this job was not worthy of a graduate of Notre Dame!

Now, having discovered what it was I wanted to do with my life, I was desperate to do it somewhere bigger than Adrian, Michigan. Whatever insecurity problems I've had, I've never been short of chutzpah. I auditioned everywhere—all the stations in Detroit, all the stations in Chicago. I'd gather my tapes and an 8 × 10 glossy and résumé together and mail them off full of fear and hope. And I'd usually receive a return letter with a salutation "Dear Mr. Donovan." When I saw an ad in *Broadcasting* magazine for WHIO radio and TV, Cox Broadcasting in Dayton, I thought, Well, it's not Gotham, but what the hell, and fired off the package. The day I received the telegram from news director Tom Frawley requesting an interview remains one of the biggest days in my life. I found out later that I was chosen because, of more than one hundred hopefuls who applied, I was the only one who sent an interview. All the other applicants offered recorded newscasts: "Good evening. In the news tonight, President Eisenhower . . ." like singing in the shower. I sent in an interview I'd done with the captain on the first ship to come down the St. Lawrence Seaway into the Great Lakes.

My first assignment at WHIO in Dayton was to sign on radio at 5:00 A.M. with the morning D.J., Lou Emm, do the newscasts on the hour and the half hour, and try to stay awake in between.

It was pretty basic stuff, but at least it wasn't just "rip and read." In between newscasts, the morning's headlines and what for a city boy was something brand-new, the livestock report, I'd call every police department in southwestern Ohio. "Any fatals?" I'd ask.

"Naw, just a couple of P.D.s."

I didn't want P.D.s (property-damage accidents). I wanted "fatals—gimme fatals."

"Sorry," the police officer would say, sensitive to my disappointment.

Lou Emm was the first "man" disc jockey I'd ever met. Everyone else had always been just a kid. He was and is to this day the Johnny Carson of the morning in Dayton, Ohio. Number One, the most successful, highest-paid D.J. in Dayton's history. And I was the kid. The new kid, at that, and I needed the job. But every day I was getting subliminal signs that Lou Emm didn't like me. Some weren't so subliminal. One day I was late for work, and while I was barreling down Shoyer Road at 5:05 A.M. I heard Lou Emm come on the air saying, "This is the morning show with Lou Emm and Willy Buck, our engineer, and newsman Phil Donahue, *if he makes it.*" How could he do that to me? He was the guy with the ratings and the clout. I was the guy with no power and a pregnant wife. More growth for Little Philly —in little bits and pieces. I am realizing that on more than one occasion in his life a man is going to want to say, "Take this job and shove it."

I had grown up with the message that all I had to do to make it in America was do my job well. Work and ye shall succeed. Now I discovered the reality that I had to please "The Boss." I had to consider an apple-polishing, would-you-like-some-coffee-Boss attitude. Is the end result a nation of people who won't make waves, won't take a chance, and who say "Yes, sir" instead of "Yes, sir, but . . ."? For me the biggest shock of growing up, learning what it means to be an adult breadwinning male in America, was learning about ass kissing. I've even seen people afraid to express their own political feelings until they gingerly feel out the boss. Despite "American ingenuity," Americans, and American men in particular, continue to die younger than many of their counterparts in other "civilized" countries. I've often wondered how much of this is due to the anxieties, insecurities and ulcers brought on by having all your job eggs in somebody else's basket.

Lou Emm used to collect the things I did wrong: running ten seconds too long on a newscast; being late for work, which meant not arriving in time to read the livestock report. (Today, I wonder if any farmer in southern Ohio waited for Phil Donahue to tell him if it was a good day to take his little piggies to market. I believe the 5 A.M. *Farm Report,* like the "pause for station identification," is, for most stations, a generally ignored radio feature that stays on the air because nervous broadcast licensees are blindly following anachronistic FCC rules requiring radio service to *all segments* of the community. Every day D.J.s and reporters all over America are sleepily ripping and reading the price of barrows and gilts, and nobody is listening.)

At the end of several weeks, a long list of grievances against me was presented to WHIO management. It was crisis time. I was not confident of my ability, and in addition to the in-house "write-ups," the station's general manager was receiving complaints from advertisers that people couldn't understand me on the air. They changed my mike. They made me stand up, sit down, breathe deeper. I remember the near-terminal fear listening to how I was sounding, rather than understanding what I was reading about Eisenhower's last days in office. This was my first introduction to the meaning of power on the job, or lack of it. Just how much courage is the new kid in town supposed to have? I had signed a year's lease on an apartment at $110 a month; I had a pregnant wife and a tiny baby; I had a Chevy Bel Air and a note that said I owed the General Motors Acceptance Corporation $96 a month for 36 months; I was making $6,700 a year. It was a crash course in job politics.

Finally I left the pigs behind for on-the-street TV reporting and, eventually, anchoring the evening news. There were some scoops—and three more babies—in those years, but my proudest accomplishment came when my right hand got on the *CBS Evening News* with Walter Cronkite. (I had yet to make it above the wrist on a network newscast.)

Arkansas Senator John McClellan and the Senate rackets committee were after Jimmy Hoffa. So was every reporter in the country. I had him staked out at the Biltmore Hotel in Dayton and waited three or four hours before he finally came out and I was able to grab an interview on the run. That night on the *CBS Evening News* with Walter Cronkite, a hand bobbing in the corner of TV screens all over America, holding a microphone to Hoffa's face, belonged to young Philly Donahue.

A second time my hand made the *CBS Evening News* was another grab-it-or-lose-it interview. This time with Billy Sol Estes. The whole national press was after him, but nobody thought to look at a certain church revival in Dayton. I went to the house of the minister with our little camera and a four-hundred-foot film magazine. I'm sure Billy was thinking, Here we are in the middle of nowhere—Dayton, Ohio— why not? The cameraman cued me.

"Do you think you will go to jail? . . . Why are you speaking in a church? . . . What are your credentials to speak in a church?" The former adviser to the President didn't know what the word "credentials" meant. I said, boldly, "No one is going to ask *me* to speak in a church." He said something about having gone to Bible college. We filmed two and a half minutes. It doesn't sound like much, but it was precious time that nobody else in the whole universe had. When I phoned CBS in New York, they couldn't believe somebody from Dayton (or was it Akron?) had found Estes. They called back and asked if I could get the film on a plane. I remember the pride, the squared shoulders, as I handed it over at the airport. And I still remember the goose bumps the next night seeing my own right hand, right there on the *CBS Evening News* with Walter Cronkite. Boy, was I proud!

The next day my phone rang at home and a woman's voice said, "Mr. Donahue, Mr. Cronkite would like to speak to you." I couldn't believe it.

"Phil, that was a goddamned good interview you sent us yesterday. If you get anything else you think we can use, call me personally."

"Thank you, Walter." (I actually called him Walter!)

I immediately (and I do mean immediately) typed up the résumé, found an 8 × 10 glossy of the face attached to that right hand and sent it air special to CBS News in New York. It was weeks before I came down from Walter's phone call, and even longer before I realized that CBS News had not answered my résumé and was not going to hire this "goddamned good" interviewer from Dayton, Ohio.

Okay, so CBS wasn't ready for me. At least the complaints about the mush-mouthed morning newsman had stopped. I was winning respect as a street reporter and news anchor, and I thought I was learning what to do as a journalist. Looking back now, I realize that one of the things I was doing was violating journalism's first commandment—thou shalt not be used.

Management asked me to host a show highlighting Dayton's largest employer—Wright Patterson Air Force Base. The base was the nearest outpost of the United States Government, and therefore, in the paranoid mind of a TV licensee, the nearest relative of the Federal Communications Commission. The show, *Technology for Tomorrow,* was an interesting example of how local TV's bottom line is "Please renew our license, Massa." It was also an example of selling the Pentagon, a widespread broadcasting practice my heroes at CBS were to document several years later. Once a month *Technology for Tomorrow* showcased "Wright Patt," as the locals called it. *Technology for Tomorrow* was a half-hour commercial for the civilian contractors who developed the new weapons systems and the military bosses who managed the projects.

Dayton was the perfect example of Eisenhower's Military-Industrial Complex. The civilians from the offices of the prime contractors had opened-ended expense accounts, and the generals freely took advantage of their invitations. And when the generals retired they went to work for the contractors. What is important here is that Yours Truly failed to say anything about the unholy alliance that good ol' Ike, a war hero, already had warned us about. Instead, I was producing nothing less than a rah-rah report on the "wonderful work being done by General Dynamics, North American, Boeing and the hardworking generals at Wright Patterson."

No one sold the Pentagon more enthusiastically and with greater vigor than Phil Donahue. I produced shows on the B-70 in which I said, "You can drive a jeep through the intakes of this aircraft—that's how big this is." And this was before it had even been flown! I did a show on the Phantom II—the F-4, which was widely used in Vietnam and is still the mainstay of military arsenals around the world. The F-4 is a sophisticated fighter-bomber which carries bombs, rockets and other "goodies," as we called these instruments that killed men, women and children. When they load this plane down, it looks like a cow with extra udders, and it can land on an aircraft carrier. To sex up the show, I obtained McDonnell Aircraft film (for free, of course) which showed the F-4 plane coming in on a low incendiary-bomb run. It came in slow, and then a tremendous flame flashed across the screen. I dubbed in the sound of the explosion. It was the most exciting damn thing you've ever seen in your life, and while I didn't realize it then, I was actually producing movies like the ones at the Riverside Theater that had made me proud to be an American. I flew to St. Louis and interviewed McDonnell president David Lewis and reported he was just an ordinary guy doing his job. "He even eats in the employees' cafeteria." I made David Lewis the Renaissance Man of prime defense contractors.

The closest I ever came to asking an embarrassing question was during an interview with one of the generals who managed the development of a fighter plane. "General," I said, "why do we have to build an F-100, an F-101, an F-102, 104, 105 and so on? Isn't this unnecessarily expensive?" The general smiled, just like on the JOIN THE AIR FORCE poster, and said that obsolescence "in this business comes very fast, and we must stay ahead of the enemy." Right, I thought. Stay ahead of the enemy. Next question. What I failed to do was pursue. If I had, I probably would have discovered that all those different planes weren't necessary and the cost of developing them was equal to reclaiming downtown Detroit, Newark, Gary and a lot of other decaying cities.

Instead, I was up all night long (while Margie slept alone) editing film and dubbing sound effects, and by the time the show ended . . . man, you sure were proud!

Young Philly—like scores of other reporters—never stopped to think about how much politics went into those planes. You couldn't give Boeing the B-70; it had just had the B-52. General Dynamics was awarded the TFX—the swing-wing job that had so much trouble. General Dynamics is located in Fort Worth, Texas, and you've got thousands of jobs at stake there, and Lyndon Johnson from Texas was majority leader on the Hill. Who the hell is gonna take something away from General Dynamics, especially if they are about to run out of making the last airplane that we gave them? These are questions I am asking now. Not then.

Wright Patterson was also AFLC—Air Force Logistics Command—the headquarters for all the hardware and all the solid-state equipment in all the black boxes on all the U.S. Government airplanes around the world. In effect, a gigantic warehouse operation—the most staggering display of computers you've ever seen in your life.

In addition to these two major areas at Wright Patt, we had a Strategic Air Command base. My job was to "key in" with the cooperation of the P.R. people and show Dayton the wonderful work being done at Wright Patterson Air Force Base, right here in our own community. It was called a public-service show.

I recall one installment on the "rough riders"—the crews who would ride into hurricanes and tornadoes in fighter planes, measure the intensity of the thunderbolts and the hail, and then come back alive to tell us about it. We showed the nose of the airplane and the dents where the hail had hit and cracked the windshield. And I'd say, "Major Highrider, what's it like in there?" and he'd say, "It's like being inside a washing machine," and everybody would say *Geeez!* It was really great stuff, boy; these guys were going in there and learning about weather, and weren't they brave people, flying into storms like that?

One of my biggest thrills was interviewing Jumpin' Joe Kissinger. Joe Kissinger took a balloon to an altitude of 101,000 feet over New

Mexico and jumped out of the thing. He free-fell in his space suit for something like 3½ minutes before his chute opened.

"What was it like?"

"I was on my back and I looked up and it was at night and all I could see was the stars. Stars don't twinkle, you know; the reason you think they twinkle is because you see the atmosphere between you and the stars."

The film showed his body fall away from the gondola and then the chute open and then the landing. He took off his helmet, and they gave him a cap and he tipped it proudly. Later he got introduced on the *Ed Sullivan Show*. "In our audience tonight is one of the most courageous Americans . . . Captain Joseph Kissinger." God, he got such an ovation!

Compared with the astronauts who would later make America proud, Jumpin' Joe was small potatoes. But his jump had a lot going for it—the balloon, the gondola, the suspense (will he make it?) . . . It wasn't Lindbergh, but it was all I had. It's hard to make this point without sounding cruel, but nowadays I look back and wonder what the hell did Joe Kissinger discover for us? It could be argued that the Kissinger balloon jump did help to improve the space suit, because it was a test in an oxygenless atmosphere, and the space suit in fact developed a leak. But you can do that in a simulator. You don't have to go out to New Mexico and jump from 101,000 feet. It was a lot of time, a lot of meetings, a lot of machismo, a lot of theatrics, a lot of press coverage, a lot of hero making, and a lot of public money, but basically it added up to not much more than good theater. And there was Donahue, the reporter, selling front-row tickets to this show. Nobody was prouder of going on television with Jumpin' Joe Kissinger than I was. The man *really* fascinated me. I even tried to get on CBS and Walter Cronkite, something I recalled with a goodly amount of chagrin some years later when I saw CBS's documentary *The Selling of the Pentagon*.

I remember walking down those long halls at Wright Patterson Air Force Base and noticing that there were a lot of people out there eating apples—literally, eating apples—and doing nothing. I didn't recognize the waste while I was there. It was only years later, with the war and Nixon and Johnson and the lies and the government and the military-industrial complex and the sudden recognition that I worked for Avco, which made bombs at its ordnance division in Richmond, Indiana, and helicopter engines, that my head started to turn. I began to realize that the kid in Chicago's Grant Park in 1968 with the headband and the peace symbol was right: wealthy men do indeed get wealthier on war. I wasn't the critical, enlightened journalist saying, "Why?" I was perpetuating a system that provided jobs for Dayton and better business for the television station. I was cheerleading for the generals, and my management was paying for the film and the union overtime because generals talked to Washington and in television we always gotta have our license renewed.

In 1960, reporter/cameraman Andy Cassells and I covered the West Virginia primary for WHIO-TV. Hubert Humphrey traveled the state in a chartered bus which bore a huge sign proclaiming OVER THE HUMP WITH HUMPHREY. By the end of that campaign you began to wonder if it would make it over the next hill. John Kennedy flew around the state in his own Convair, named *Caroline*. Hubert had a man named Jimmy Wakely who played guitar and sang folk songs at all the campaign stops; J.F.K. came in with a sound truck and Frank Sinatra recordings about "Kennedy All the Way." I remember Hubert saying he felt like the corner store running against the big chain operation. Here was this good ol' country-boy druggist running against the man who always had a Nassau tan. When Kennedy smiled, he looked like every penny of his millions—all you could see was teeth. Hubert looked like a dollar ninety-eight. And Kennedy knew how to handle the press. We were packing up our camera gear one morning at a plant gate and he walked over and said, "Thanks for coming with us," and I thought, Hey, what a nice guy (Irish Catholic, too). He went out of his way to come over and thank us, the nobodies. That was my first experience with media manipulation by a political candidate.

Kennedy was nominated. The campaign was in full swing when "WHIO newsman Phil Donahue" got permission to interview Vice-President Nixon. It was in a private car in a campaign train in Springfield, Ohio. I was nervous. The Secret Service was all over the place. There we were in Nixon's compartment with the shades drawn, and outside thousands were waiting for the candidate to appear. I said, "Mr. Vice-President, may we interview Mrs. Nixon?" He agreed. I was scared to death. "Mrs. Nixon, you've had a number of proud moments in your life . . ." and when I said "proud" I spat right in her eye. You can see it on the film. She recoiled. To this day I feel a real debt to Mrs. Nixon. She could have said, "Hey, you spat in my eye." But like a trooper she just continued smiling. (I believe it's very important for every citizen to exercise the right to vote, not only because

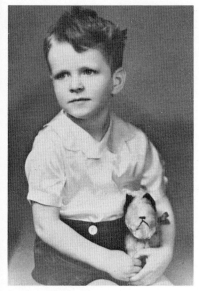

1. The author at three.

2. At 10 with my sister Kathy, 5.

3. Graduation from St. Edward High School, Cleveland, 1953.

4. Uncle Jim McClory, my sister Kathy, "The Graduate," Mom and Dad at graduation from Notre Dame, 1957.

5. Then . . .
"The Gang" at Notre Dame,
1953. My roommate, "Good Ol'
George," is next to me. (I'm
holding the baseball bat.)

6. Now. . .
"The Gang" with wives and Sophia Loren on my set—October 26, 1979. That's George
behind the actress.

7. The Grotto at Notre Dame.

8. Church of the Incarnation, Centerville, Ohio.

9. Celebrating Dan's sixth birthday—April 17, 1967. The children, left to right: Mary Rose; Brenda, a foster child who lived with us for a year; Dan; Mike; Kevin; Jim.

10. Family day at the Ohio State Fair—August 1970. Left to right: me, Mary Rose, Mike, Dan, Kevin, Jim, Margie.

11. Mary Rose Donahue, dressed in antebellum costume for a scene we taped on the Grand Staircase of the *Mississippi Queen* riverboat during a remote week, with her proud father — December 1977.

12. The Donahue "men" at a Variety Club party honoring the show's 10th anniversary — March 7, 1978. Left to right: Jim, Kevin, me, Dan, Mike.

13. A dark-haired Phil Donahue—my first "8×10 glossy" for *The Phil Donahue Show*, 1967.

14. Examining the electric chair at the Ohio State Penitentiary with Dick Mincer, Executive Producer of *The Phil Donahue Show*, who refused to touch it. We taped one week of shows from inside the prison—November 1971.

15. Don Dahlman, then General Manager of WLW-D in Dayton, greeting John T. Murphy, President of Avco Broadcasting Corporation, arriving in Dayton.

16. With Richard Nixon and Herb Klein at the White House—July 27, 1972. Where's Margie?

17. Marlo on *Donahue* — January 26, 1977.

18. Interviewing Erma Bombeck, author, TV commentator, syndicated columnist and my former neighbor in Centerville — San Diego, March 1, 1978.

it's a great constitutional privilege, but out of compassion for what the candidates and their families go through.)

During this heady exposure to national politics, I gained some other insights. I was constantly bumping into network reporters, the Olympians of the trade, and recall them being very cynical and having very little time for local yokels. If I would say something like "Excuse me, sir, do you know if Mr. Kennedy will be going on to Huntington from here?" I'd get "You tell me, pal. You tell me, you win the cigar, kid." Network people always seemed a little too fast and a little too impersonal. But then in my freshmanitis, I had nothing but respect and awe for those larger-than-life people who worked for the networks, traveled with the President, had their own press plane and made the edit decisions that determined what 100 million American people saw each night on the news. And—if they were reporters, they got their hand *and their face* on the *CBS Evening News*. I felt lucky to get forty seconds on the air in Dayton.

After the election I covered Kennedy's first Presidential visit to Ohio, a fund raiser for Governor Mike DiSalle. I was at the airport when he landed. There were the two planes, *Air Force One,* also nicknamed *Caroline,* and the press plane. It was raining like hell, and I ran for shelter under the wing, where I stood right next to Roger Mudd. What the hell, I thought, I'll just take a look inside and see how the big guys travel. So "Mr. Dayton, Ohio" walks onto the press plane, and I'm thinking, Boy, oh boy, oh boy, this is it, The Press. This is *The New York Times*. This is NBC, CBS, ABC—this is *everybody*.

Later I would wonder, can a reporter fly around in what is for all practical purposes a jet-powered gilded cage with an open bar and be in touch with the America 35,000 feet below? And if you are really in the press *élite*—riding in *Air Force One* and eating chicken-salad sandwiches with the President—can you retain objectivity? If Woodward and Bernstein had been White House correspondents, would Nixon have been forced to resign?*

And if power corrupts politicians, can it corrupt the press as well? If in order to maintain a viable democracy we must change Presidents every eight years, shouldn't *Time* magazine relieve Hugh Sidey after ten? (Ben Bradlee has been editing *The Washington Post* for nearly two decades.)

* The danger of the reporter being seduced by the powerful people he covers is not exclusive to Washington, D.C. During a meeting with former Chicago Mayor Michael A. Bilandic in his City Hall office, he told me that the City Hall reporters were "great guys." It was "these investigative types" that bothered him.

In the summer of 1972, five years after *The Phil Donahue Show* premiered, a telegram arrived at the Donahue house: "The President and Mrs. Nixon request the pleasure . . ." The men who really requested the pleasure of our company were Ehrlichman and Haldeman, who had probably decided that those network liberals didn't like the President or his men. There is no White House tape, but here's my re-creation of a conversation that led to the sending of invitations to local reporters and personalities: "Dan Rather and Richard Valeriani—the bastards just copy each other. They aren't our kind of people. Our kind of people are the silent majority. Our kind of people are the guys at the local level—Wally Phillips and Fahey Flynn of Chicago, Jack LeGoff of Detroit, Jim Jensen of New York City, J. P. McCarthy of Detroit—those locals are conservative."

Margie and I packed our best clothes and went to Washington. Not coincidentally, Julie Eisenhower was to be on my show the following day. Everyone who was anyone, but wasn't network, was there. There were two drinks, then no more drinks. The bar vanished. Suddenly, dum dum de dum dum. Hail to the Chief. Well, I was impressed. The crowd parted like the Red Sea and in came Pat and Dick. "We want you to feel at home here in the White House," Richard Nixon said. "Julie said just the other day, 'Dad, you have had the newspaper people here; you'd better have the television people in here in order to be fair.' And I want you to know that this house is yours to see . . . feel free to move about. I'd like you to go upstairs and see the Lincoln room, a room in which Winston Churchill slept, as has Queen Elizabeth. Of course, not at the same time." Big hand—big laugh. Perfect. And we did go upstairs and we walked around, we bounced on the Lincoln bed, we went everywhere (except the Presidential quarters). There were a few nice-looking bluecoats standing about—the kids with the short hair, the ones you'd like your daughter to bring home— but nobody hassled us.

I stood in a huge bay window upstairs and looked across the South Lawn of the White House at a group of demonstrators outside the fence. Powerless kids protesting the Vietnam war—and my vantage point was from within. I had never had that king's-eye view before; I doubt I ever will again. As I absorbed the irony, a bluecoat who looked like Tyrone Power's son commented, "White House security wanted to get rid of them, but the President said no." Get it? Your President is so tolerant of dissent he won't even permit the removal of these ill-advised young people who are not mature enough to understand that Nixon's foreign policy is good for America. What the bluecoat failed to say (or understand) was that dissenters, however power-less, however dirty their hair, however much a pain in the ass, were very much within their constitutional rights on the public sidewalk in front of the public house that symbolizes America's remarkable two-hundred-year attempt at democracy (paternalistic Presidents to the contrary notwithstanding).

At the receiving line downstairs there was a man taking pictures. At the instruction of a White House aide, I was first, Margie was second. Herb Klein was standing next to the President, and an aide gave him my name. Klein whispered my identity in Nixon's ear. "Yes," the President said, "Julie told me she is going to be on *The Phil Donahue Show* tomorrow. Well, I certainly know she'll enjoy . . ." And the man was snapping pictures like mad. While Margie was meeting the President, I was meeting Mrs. Nixon, and she asked, "Are there phone calls on your show?" I knew why she was asking. I answered, "Yes, ma'am, there are calls, but they are screened. I want to assure you we are in charge of the calls and I'm sure there'll be no nuisance calls." Translated: No calls that disagree with Julie's father will be accepted. Score another one for the White House.

And it came to pass the Phil Donahues went home to the Midwest and jokingly told their friends they were going to put NIXON'S THE ONE bumper stickers all over both their cars. We didn't, but we did talk about how easy it is to be sucked in, and how nice Nixon really is. And we were bona fide liberals! We were people who had been writing (small) checks for McGovern.

Two weeks later the White House photos came. All Phil. No Margie. She had a mother and a father and uncles and a grandmother who was 78 and going to die within the year. Was it sexist? Or just damned insensitive? Did the pictures turn out? Or did they bother to take pictures of the wives at all? I felt for Margie, a woman who was not getting much attention and who was married to a guy who was getting a lot. Despite the oversight, the Nixon campaign strategy—go-out-to-the-hinterlands-and-bring-in-these-local-guys-who-like-us-because-the-people-we've-been-letting-in-here-are-killing-us—almost worked.

At the White House that night I ran into Andy Cassells, my old cameraman from WHIO. He was on assignment with the Cox Bureau in Washington covering its local guy from Charlotte, North Carolina. Andy Cassells was the first person to ever tell me to go to hell during an assignment. I was the eager-to-be-on-Walter-Cronkite right hand, willing to stay up all night for the story; he was the guy who after we worked twenty-four straight hours on an assignment always wanted to go to bed. He was behind the camera; I was in front. Who could blame him?

One of those "go to hell" times was a mine disaster in the Appalachians. Thirty-eight miners were trapped at Holden, West Virginia; and the eager right hand and his faithful camera "crew," Andy, went. Going out of town on a story for a local news show in a market the size of Dayton was almost unheard of, but Andy and I did it.

We were snowed in on the top of the mountain near the mine entrance. We'd planned to be there for one night, but it turned out to be three nights, eating Red Cross doughnuts and urinating behind a railroad car. Meanwhile Margie, at home with two babies, ran out of money. I had to call my folks and ask them to send her $50—it was the only time since leaving home I had to do that, and it killed me. But I had suddenly become the CBS presence on the story. I was phoning in reports to New York which were being broadcast by Blair Clark, who was then the reporter on the radio network's evening newscast, *The World Tonight*. First my hand on CBS, now my voice. It was only radio, but it was CBS. I was making real progress!

The rescue teams came out of the mine, and the men had soot all over their faces. The lights on their hats and one smudge pot were the only sources of illumination. Worried relatives of the trapped miners were waiting in the snow. They all gathered around the smudge pot, and a preacher said, "Dear God, let us pray." They joined hands and began to sing.

> What a friend we have in Jesus,
> All our sins and griefs to bear!
> What a privilege to carry
> Everything to God in prayer!

One by one, everyone began singing there in the snow on the mountaintop. It gave me goose bumps. It was beautiful. I knew it would look great on film, on CBS, but our camera was freezing—the oil had thickened in the cold, and the film was dragging. Instead of a moving minute or so of prayer and softly falling snow, we would have had Charlie Chaplin–type funny, stiff-legged walking, and screechy sound. Finally I got the oil warmed by literally holding the camera against my body. I went back to the preacher. It was 2:30 in the morning, and

I was finally the personification of CBS Television. I had the camera, the film, and I was the only network there.

"Reverend, I'm from CBS News, and could you please go back through your prayer again? We have two hundred and six television stations across the country who will hear you pray for these miners." What a wonderful feeling it was to be able to say, "I'm from CBS News and I'm going to deliver several million people to you." I felt very powerful.

The minister looked at me and then said, "Son, I just couldn't do it. I have already prayed to my God, and any further praying at this time would be wrong. No, sir, I just can't do it."

I could not believe what I was hearing. I was convinced that he didn't hear me. "Reverend, I'M FROM CBS NEWS." To this day I can hear the sound of my voice saying, "CEE BEE ESS NEWS" echoing down the mountainside and through a nearby canyon.

"My report will be seen in every city in America. Please, Reverend, pray one more time so the people of the United States of America will see what a fine religious community this is and join in your prayer to save these miners. . . ."

The preacher just looked at me. He was uncomfortable, but firm. "No, sir. I have already prayed, and that's that."

I was in shock. I walked slowly to the nearest phone station, my head bowed in as big a defeat as I had ever sustained as a working reporter. I dropped a dime in the slot, called collect to CBS News in New York and, with my hand clutching the phone until my knuckles turned white, waited for the voice on the other end to accept my call. When he did, I blurted out through clenched teeth, "The son of a bitch won't pray!"

I don't know exactly when the revelation struck. It must have been a year later. I was driving to work one day and it hit me. That preacher's stand was the greatest demonstration of moral courage I had ever encountered in my life. The man would not show-biz for Jesus. He would not sell his soul for TV. Not even national TV. Not even, praise God, for CBS.

I have thought of that preacher and that night many times since. I don't know where he is now, but if he isn't going to Heaven, no one is.

Suburbia

CENTERVILLE, OHIO, is a suburb of a suburb. It grew in the early sixties when contractors moved in, bought a lot of land, surveyed it and then built scores of houses in one area, all alike. Centerville is about as far away from urban anxiety as you can get and still not have a septic tank. Bumper stickers on station wagons with wooden sides say THINK SAY AND PLAY SOCCER. The only thing open all night in Centerville is the local doughnut shop.

Centerville is where I became, for the first time in my life, a property owner. Our first house cost $16,300, and although I didn't realize it then, I had chosen a house across the street from a woman who would become a national celebrity. Her name was Erma Bombeck. Erma and I had three things in common: we were both Catholic, we both had Early American furniture and we both lived in the same kind of house.

It was 1963. My crisis caused by announcer's mush mouth was over. By now I could pronounce the letter W, as in WHIO, dub-ul-u, subtly rolling my tongue between the -ul- and the -u, unlike some far less talented local announcers who helplessly pronounced it dub-a-u. I had made my last $96 GMAC payment. My lawn, while not a prizewinner, was acceptable, and, lo and behold, we had had four kids in four years! Margie was pregnant for the fifth time; I was earning $15,000 a year, so naturally, we bought a bigger house.

House number two was a $33,000 job built by the Zengel brothers, who had inherited some Old World quality-consciousness from their

German-born father. In 1965 our daughter, Mary Rose, was born. If anybody deserved a daughter, it was Margie. She had had four children in four years, and they were all boys. She never complained, but her longing for a girl was apparent. Now we had not only a girl, but a new house, a good job with some glamour, great neighbors and two cars—one a station wagon with wooden sides. Perfect.

Not quite. At WHIO my star was rising while my time on the job as husband and father was falling. By then I was an anchorman on the 11-o'clock news and had been assigned to moderate an afternoon radio program called *Conversation Piece*. I was on radio at 1 o'clock every day, and except for a brief visit home for dinner, I wasn't finished until the end of the 11-o'clock TV news each night. When I got home at 11:45 P.M. there wasn't much to do except drink beer, eat chocolate cookies and watch the *Tonight* show. It was a life pattern that was to last until 1967, and I was pursuing it right in the middle of five small children, a lot of diapers, meals, doctor's-office visits and the beginning of a new wave of activism for an old movement. It was called Women's Liberation.

6

"I Quit."

In 1967, I took my first critical look at my professional life. I was earning almost $20,000 a year—probably more than anybody else in the news department. I was producing and moderating *Conversation Piece*—the phone-in radio show—five days a week, coanchoring the 6- and 11-o'clock news, and presiding over a daily TV business program that included a market report and an interview with a Dayton businessman who was chosen and brought to the station by a salesman for the sponsor, the Dayton Power and Light Company. These daily interviews proved to be among the most challenging of my career. How do you make the founder and president of Dayton Pneumatic Drilling and Foundry Supply interesting?

My "public personality" had been established through *Conversation Piece*. (CALLER: "Phil, I don't iron my husband's underwear. All my neighbors do. Am I remiss?") My "public face" had been established through the evening TV newscasts, and my "public connections" were being developed through all the fat-cat interviews on *Business Trends*.

By then Margie and I were being invited to dinners, cocktails and charity fund-raisers at the homes of people my children would today call "richies." I recall the thrill of standing in the spacious living room of an Oakwood home (Dayton's "old money" suburb) in an ill-fitting rented tuxedo trying to appear casual and interesting while chatting with James Cox, Jr., the son of the former governor of Ohio and 1920 presidential candidate. The fact that Mr. Cox was then the reigning chief executive and operating superdomo of the Cox Broadcasting

Company, my employer, was enough to make a guy switch from beer to bloody Marys, which I did. Later that year I gave serious thought to actually buying a tuxedo. Which I didn't—not for the next ten years.

The money was good, the wife was beautiful, the kids were healthy, the job was prestigious, but the man was miserable. And so was his wife. Margie never bought into the TV game. She didn't like my job, was not close to the people I worked with and for, and was uncomfortable with the incidental recognition she received. The fact that Margie's unhappiness grew without my even noticing it is itself evidence of my consuming professional ambition and only one indication of how little energy I was really giving to my responsibilities at home. ("Get a good wife and you've just about got a happy marriage made.") Toward the end of our marriage I recall just standing there filled with bewilderment as to how my wife had "suddenly" become so very unhappy.

I always believed Margie was the best-looking wife at the party—any party. (Much later I would think about "appearance values" and what a major role they played in the lives of so many people and how in the final rendering "pretty" had nothing to do with anything—except stroking the ego of the macho man who takes the "little woman" out only to "show her off.") I was *proud* of Margie, not because she was a good mother (which she was), not because she was a good homemaker (which she was—though all women were supposed to be that) but because she was pretty. Being pretty was not expected of every woman, and not every guy was expected to get a pretty one. Only the guys with gumption. And so after a day of interviewing the latest V.I.P. to visit our area and delivering the news "compiled and edited in the WHIO Central News Bureau" and moving about in my professional world as if I really knew what I was doing, at night I was escorting Margie to social events. While she was obviously beautiful, what was not so obvious (to me) was that my "pretty little woman" was developing a very serious case of resentment born out of diapers and dishes and being married to Dayton's Mr. Television.

And while Margie and Phil were not, as they say at Esalen, "sharing feelings with each other," she was sharing *hers* with many wives in the neighborhood, every day and usually on the telephone. (An ashtray filled with half-smoked Kent cigarettes could usually be found next to the phone.) The resentments emerged not in a torrent, but in small cloudbursts. "Your idea of fatherhood is throwing a ball at the boys," she would say. And I would respond the way I always responded, to everything—I would talk, often too much and too critically. Margie had no enthusiasm for long arguments about the "malaise" that had settled over our marriage. She knew an "argument" meant that I did most of the talking; and most of my comments were critical, usually delivered with a "how-come-you-can't-see-this" look on my face. Margie felt like Eliza Doolittle and I felt like the not-so-"Quiet Man" who couldn't get his wife to argue back.

We both felt trapped. Regardless, I still had gumption—and remained ambitious. However, I knew that as far as WHIO was concerned, I had gone as far as I was going to go. I had always measured success in terms of the size of the city in which I worked. Cleveland was the big time, but I had failed in my effort to stay there. Now I wanted the big time again. My fantasy was to work in a city with two airports.

I found television news anchoring boring—especially the late news, which was nothing more than a rewrite of the early news unless you got "lucky" with a *good* fire. My enthusiasm was dying as my job became routine. "Good evening, everyone. Here's the news for Schoenling beer," and "The Dayton Power and Light Company, your investor-owned company, presents *Business Trends*. Tonight's guest is Emmert Royer, president of BHA Pianos and Organs . . ." (Much later I wondered why a utility, a monopoly, spent so much money advertising, when the customers couldn't go anywhere else for service anyway.)

I wanted out. I wanted out and up. I wanted KMOX in St. Louis, WGN in Chicago, WBZ in Boston or WJR in Detroit. I wanted to do *Conversation Piece* on a 50-thousand-watter. I wanted to interrupt the program and read the weather forecast with *two* different current temperatures at two different airports or at least two different locations, like the "western suburbs" or "along the lake."

I sent my audition tapes everywhere. And from everywhere they came back, accompanied by a mimeographed letter with my name written into the salutation, gently worded but always the same: "We've hired someone else." And so, in June 1967, nervously clinging to a belief that the world was filled with people who could not make a decision, I walked into my boss's office and said, "I quit." He couldn't have been more surprised. Nor could I.

My next job was with the E. F. MacDonald Co., an incentive and trading-stamp firm headquartered in Dayton. The company is a multi-million-dollar worldwide corporation that offers travel and merchandise to sales personnel, franchised dealers, gas-station attendants, bank tellers and other people in the marketplace as an incentive to encourage more sales, reduce job accidents, develop new business or otherwise propose new and profitable ideas. Checks for prize points are issued to achieving contest participants, who may redeem them for merchandise shown in the attractive E. F. MacDonald catalog or for fancy vacation trips almost anywhere.

My starting salary was $17,500 per year. Despite the cut in pay, the hours were regular, and for the first time in more than five years I was, thanks to God and Scott's fertilizer and lawn seed, enjoying my home in the evening. Being a normal person was wonderful!

For about three months.

My responsibilities with E. F. MacDonald were unusually important for a beginning salesman. My celebrity status earned me a spot on the sales team that was planning a huge trip to Hawaii for Frigidaire dealers who met or exceeded quotas during the sales contest. I also called on Marathon Oil in Findlay, Ohio, another large and important account. MacDonald accounts usually totaled in the millions. This was big-league business, and I was determined to make good at it.

My travels up and down Interstate 75 in western Ohio exposed me to the often lonely and anxiety-ridden life of the modern salesman. I sat in industrial lobbies with him, and watched as he gave his business card to the receptionist and waited for Mr. Big—not hoping for an immediate sale, just for the chance to pitch him. I saw secretaries come out of hallways and from behind huge metal doors and say, "I'm sorry, he won't be able to see you today." When the salesmen left, I wondered where they went and I thought about how much their livelihoods were determined by a fickle economy over which they had no control. I thought about their security and their emotional well-being.

In the vast arena that we call "business," there is no more risky or ego-smashing activity than what salesmen know as "the cold call." Nothing else measures a man's spirit or ability or gumption so much as walking in to a prospective customer for the first time, unannounced, and requesting an opportunity to pitch Mr. Big. Usually the salesman is as welcome as a Jehovah's Witness at the front door. Nevertheless, most "account executives" worth their expense reports will tell you, like the people who work at the morgue, "Somebody's got to do it."

On one such call, I presented my card to the receptionist in the huge lobby of the Copeland Refrigeration Company on I-75 north of Dayton. The firm supplies industrial products worldwide, and I had it figured for a potential $1 million per year in incentive business. (I wasn't sure why, but everyone else at MacDonald's always spoke in seven figures, so naturally I did too.) As I sat waiting for the vice-president in charge of marketing to clear his office for me, the receptionist looked across the large shiny tile floor and said, "I'll never understand why you left such an exciting job to do this."

Almost immediately a young woman not older than 18 appeared, walked over to where I was pretending to read an *Iron Age* magazine and said, "Mr. Bennett is busy. What do you have to show me?"

Undaunted, and convinced that the best salesmen are the ones who keep going in spite of adversity, I decided next time to play my ace. I was a celebrity; I had social connections, and now I was going to use them to make some noise in the executive offices of my new company. I made a cold call on Phillips Industries, a company that manufactured window framing for the millions of recreation vehicles and mobile homes all over the world. If ever there was a company that could use the E. F. MacDonald service, it was this one. And it was headed by Jesse Phillips, a man whose personal company I had enjoyed while a WHIO celebrity.

When I walked into the lobby, it was filled with other salesmen who had already presented their calling cards and were sitting back with copies of *Metal Working Weekly*, awaiting the appearance of their contact. I presented my card to the receptionist and said, loud enough for everyone to hear, "Mr. Donahue to see Mr. Phillips." The woman looked at me only briefly, examined the card and asked me to take a seat.

For thirty minutes I waited.

Finally Jesse Phillips appeared in a doorway and looked across the lobby at me. It was immediately apparent that he had no idea who I was. And as the other salesmen looked over the tops of their magazines, Jesse Phillips locked eyes with me and said, "We don't use *incentives* here."

Meanwhile, across town, the general manager of Avco Broadcasting's WLW-D, Dayton's only other VHF television station, himself a former salesman, was about to make a "cold call." Mr. Dahlman made his pitch at lunch. Johnny Gilbert, a popular singer/variety-show host, was leaving WLW-D for Hollywood, and Dahlman was looking for a replacement. What did I think about doing a show like *Conversation Piece* on television?

Four lunches later—and after a promise that I would not have to anchor the 11-o'clock news and a guarantee of $24,000 during the first year of a two-year contract (I had never in my life been offered a contract)—I sheepishly discussed the deal with Margie. She reluctantly said, "It's your decision," and even more sheepishly I offered my resignation at E. F. MacDonald.

7
Phases

MY JOB change wasn't the only life change I was experiencing in 1967.

In addition to soccer and lawns, we found one other focal point in Centerville. It was called the Church of the Incarnation. Its pastor was Father Raymond Kallaher. He ran the church, the school and the weekly raffle. The school was just about paid for when a Chicago firm was engaged to conduct a parish-wide fund drive aimed at raising money for a new church building. The old structure was Christmas-card pretty, white steeple and all, but very small and very inadequate for the rapidly growing community of Catholics in Centerville.

The professional fund raisers were very slick—bearing pledge cards, suggested sales pitch, artist's rendering of the proposed church and the line "stewardship for the Lord." First, a small group of parish insiders were invited to a preliminary meeting to discuss the money-raising effort. Next, invitations were sent to parish men (not women), who would work in pairs and go door to door soliciting pledges from the faithful. These were the grunts, the men in the trenches, on whose shoulders the entire effort would rest. I was a grunt. My partner was a former University of Dayton basketball player named Bill Uhl. The time by then was the late sixties, and America was in crisis. Blacks were burning cities, and slowly, very slowly, a whole lot of people were beginning to wonder whether the Vietnam war was a good idea.

Enter Donahue, the TV guy, the white liberal, in all his Phase One glory. Phase One is the fun phase of a four-phase package of commitment, the phase in which a liberal says to himself, Hey, where've I been? There's work to be done, problems to be solved, poor to be fed. And I can do it. Phase One liberals develop their first relationships with black people. They enjoy being seen with minorities, mastering the fancy handshake, getting yuks in interracial groups with on-color jokes. However fanciful, unenlightened and counter-productive the phase, most white liberals had to go through it. It was hard to grow without first passing out cookies to the "colored" kids, patting their heads and feeling pumped up at finally having relationships with the people who previously had either collected your garbage or been running backs for the Cleveland Browns.

Phase One was fun! "Right on, brother!"

But Phase One and the parish fund drive were like oil and water for me. How could I help raise money for what would probably be a million-dollar church when the needs of "the least of His brethren" were not being met? Much later, I would wonder about the arrogance of the oft-repeated pulpit euphemism "least of His brethren." Did this mean *we* were "the most of His brethren?" The questions came very fast. Is God more interested in stained-glass windows than in people? With Watts and Detroit and Newark burning, should the predominantly white suburb of Centerville be building a seven-figure building that, in an age of changing liturgy, might be obsolete in just a few years? Yes, we needed a church, but did it have to be an architectural monument? My answer in each case was no, and although I didn't know it then, my life, my faith, my attitude toward my country and my church, and my marriage would never be the same again.

Within weeks I pulled out of the fund drive, leaving Bill Uhl to work the neighborhood all by his seven-foot self. A group of close friends who also believed that Jesus was not interested in million-dollar buildings suddenly became even closer. It was a good thing we had the companionship, because we were going to need it.

The four couples who led the charge against Church tradition and the archdiocesan "edifice complex" were Jim and Maddi Breslin, Frank and Pat Swift, Roberta and Eddie Fisher, and Phil and Marge Donahue. Fisher and Breslin were Xavier graduates; Swift was from the University of Dayton. Among us we had twenty kids. How do you like your Catholics?

Our purpose was to halt plans for the big church and steer the Incarnation community into a less expensive yet practical building. We had no figure in mind, but we probably would have settled on a half-million-dollar structure.

First, we tried selling our ideas at open meetings. "If Jesus landed at the Dayton airport and we placed Him in a limousine and took Him to Centerville and showed Him our new church, He would probably say, 'Yes, but what are you doing for my less fortunate people in the inner city?' " Hokey? Probably, but we believed in the rightness of our position. Most of the parishioners who attended, however, were not sure what we were talking about. Several wanted the church to "look nice" and be "in keeping with the neighborhood." Then the reaction set in.

Some parishioners wanted to know if we thought Jesus should be "worshiped in a grass hut." Several wanted to know what we spent on booze. Still others were convinced I was involved in the protest in order to promote my recently premiered talk show on WLW-D in Dayton. Begin Phase Two.

Phase Two is the angry phase. Everybody's a bigot but you. No one understands the problem quite as clearly as you. Phase Two–ers turn people off. Righteous indignation abounds in the Phase Two community. "Colored" is changed to "black," and racial jokes are taboo.

I ran for parish council and I won. I replaced Erma Bombeck (who had moved out of the parish) as head of the communications committee. My job was to edit and publish a parish newspaper. Four little girls had been killed in a Birmingham bombing, Martin Luther King had been assassinated and this angry Phase Two liberal was serving on the parish council, organizing an integrated summer camp for kids (Camp Dakota) and serving on the board of the Dakota Street Center, an activities house founded by a Marianist priest, Fr. Philip Hoelle, from the University of Dayton. It was situated in the middle of Dayton's black ghetto. It was here, during the board meetings featuring white and black members, that I got my first lesson in paternalism. One: the whites did all the talking; and two: they made most of the recommendations regarding policy. I recall suggesting that we appeal to Goodwill for some badly needed furniture for the center. One of the black members of the board replied, "Hell, we *give* stuff to Goodwill." Massa Donahue still had some growing to do.

I learned a lot during my Phase Two experience, both as a liberal serving on the parish council and as a board member of the Dakota Street Center. I learned about the inefficiency of handout programs, about the dominance of the white men, even the well-intentioned ones, and about the importance of preserving the dignity of those who receive the handouts. I learned about a schizophrenic white America that gave itself goose pimples and busted its buttons with the pride of

Christmas fund drives and then in almost the same breath condemned poor people for being on the dole.

America was in the middle of one of the most cataclysmic times of change in its history. Cities were burning, blacks were enraged, Catholics were defying the Pope and using birth control *anyway,* and women of all faiths were beginning to wonder about the male establishment. (It was about this time that I noticed that some of the women in our protest group had stopped going to Sunday Mass. The women were first.) And as if all this were not enough, we were in the throes of the worst foreign debacle in the history of the republic—the Vietnam war. And I was standing there in the midst of it all, while all the "absolutes" of my childhood were suddenly under siege.

A few years earlier on my call-in radio program *Conversation Piece,* I had interviewed Martin Luther King, Malcolm X and college professors against the war. Meanwhile, we and our friends in Centerville were busing our children to an inner-city Catholic school because we firmly believed it was an effective way to insure kids against the evil of racism. We met with the bishop and the nuns at the downtown school and the vice-president of the bus company, and as usual, the whites did most of the talking. The program was voluntary, and of course, the participants were few in number.

The decision to bus followed hours of agonizing over the manner of our own upbringing and a cold evaluation of how Holy Mother Church in good ol' North America actually compounds the problem.

I recall countless evenings when the dissident busers and naysayers would sit around someone's family room and, as the beer flowed, we would all rail about the "isms" that were the result of our Catholic upbringing.

— Racism: Jesus was white, all his followers were white, the nuns were white, the monsignor who ran the parish was white, even the guardian angel who helped us over old rickety bridges was white. All the statues in the church were white. Now, come on (we argued), there's no way to get out of this without having at least traces of racism in the Catholic soul.

— Sexism: God the FATHER; His SON; Peter, the Head of His Church, and all those folks at the Last Supper were you-know-what. The nuns, who got a bad case of clammy hands whenever Father visited our classroom, were not permitted inside the altar rail during Mass. The boy children they sacrificed their whole lives to teach were summoned to *serve* Mass. Women did "women's work": cleared the altar of soiled linen, mended the priests' garments, pushed and pulled young acolytes into a straight line before they entered the sanctuary during midnight Mass, stood meekly off to the side while the regal men who had been ordained (a sacrament) turned to the congregation at the end of the Mass, stretched out their arms as though to fly and with white expensive fabric flowing majestically from their shoulders sang, *"Ita . . . aaa . . . aaa . . . mis ah est"* ("Go, the mass is ended"). Very grand, very theatrical, very impressive. And all the time countless young children not only at Our Lady of the Angels in Cleveland, but at Masses all over the world, were looking on, and they were receiving a very simple message: Men lead; women serve.

During Phase Two, I used every speaking opportunity I could to condemn the Church for what I was convinced were her errant ways. I castigated the Dayton Catholic Women's Club for its "lily-whiteness." I condemned the "silent sisters" for not speaking out and for "being more concerned about the length of their habits than about the fact that Catholics were raising another generation of racists." For too many nuns, I said, obedience was not a vow, but an excuse not to get involved. Mr. Angry in all his self-righteousness was rolling.

It was a time for panels—usually the rabbi, the priest and the minister. High school gyms were crowded with suspicious white suburbanites, concerned but anxious and always feeling a little guilty. Finally I graduated from moderator (which I hated) to participant (which I loved). While other panel members droned on about our "responsibility to our brothers whether they be black, white, green or blue, " I went for specifics:

> Eeny, meeny, miny, mo,
> Catch a nigger by the toe.

The line awakened everybody, and I went on to say that that limerick was as much a part of my childhood as "Mary had a little lamb." My point was that we all had come out of a racist environment and that the time had come to realize that none of us could claim to have completely escaped it. Racism, I said, was a lot like cancer, in that you didn't always know you had it. I concluded by saying that you couldn't correct something if you didn't acknowledge that it was there. "Far too many people are in the full-time business of denying they have it," I said. (Light applause.)

Throughout the Phase Two stage and the busing, and the challenging of the church building and trying to find used furniture for the Dakota Street Center, I recall my own inner conflict about black people. I remember my conscience tugging at me on the issue of race. How did I *really* feel about black people? Would I want my daughter to marry one? I bused my boys; would I bus my daughter? What about being first in the neighborhood to sell my house to a black family?

The civil rights crisis was not the only cause of my anxiety. Every week at least one hundred of the nation's finest young men were returning home from Southeast Asia in plastic zipper bags. I was 32; they were 22. I missed the chance to get killed in a war by accident of birth. Not only had I not been drafted: I had never even served in the reserves. I recall wondering what turns my career might have taken had I been obliged to take a military time-out for two years. I felt guilty because I was busy gathering broadcasting experience while other young men were shooting it out with the Cong.

Imagine my dilemma when I met Matt Thompson. Matt was head of the American Friends Service Committee for Dayton and espoused the Quaker position on pacifism better than anyone I had ever met. He was a middle-aged man with all the commitment of the young "peaceniks," but without the headband, tie-dyed T-shirt and long hair. He was a politically savvy person who desperately wanted the Vietnam war to end. More desperately, he wanted the United States out of Indochina. He stated his case without rancor and without the vulgar rhetoric of the angry students who gathered for peace rallies in the late sixties. Matt Thompson was a dove whom grandmothers could love. I often called him when I needed the liberal antiwar position represented on *Conversation Piece*.

Every Wednesday, Matt and other Quakers would stand at the corner of 2nd and Ludlow in downtown Dayton. They didn't march, they didn't sing, they didn't say anything. They just stood there. Some held signs which said STOP THE WAR. Their vigil was a powerfully silent one and, for me, a distracting reminder of all those plastic zipper bags. I remember wondering how many of the bags contained bodies of young men who could have moderated *Conversation Piece* better than I, and I remember the conflict I felt with the realization that they would never get the chance.

The first civil rights confrontation I had ever seen had happened in Yellow Springs, Ohio, in the early sixties. Scores of Antioch College students sat down in front of Lewis Gegner's barbershop in Xenia because he refused to serve blacks. He said he wasn't trained to cut Negro hair. Sheriff's deputies used tear gas to break up the protest.

Matt Thompson's demonstration was different. Here six to eight middle-aged adults (both men and women) simply bore silent witness. I had tremendous admiration for those quiet, sincere, civil, gentle protestors. The kids in Yellow Springs may have been more courageous, but the Quakers' silent vigil had a greater effect on me. I told Matt how I felt, and he said, "Phil, why don't you join us?" And I said, "Gee, Matt . . ."

All I would have had to do was stand there. No marching, no chanting, no obscenities, no hymns, no pamphlets, no nothing. Just stand there. But I couldn't do it. I never joined them.

I had begun to question whether it was right for me, a journalist, to make a public statement of protest about a matter on which I would be reporting on the 11-o'clock news. Would Roger Mudd join in if the protest took place in Washington? Would James Reston march on the White House? How much of my guilt was caused by concern over professional objectivity and how much by cowardice? Had Walter Cronkite surrendered his credentials as a citizen when he chose a career as a reporter? One hundred plastic zipper bags a week! Was the issue professional virginity or staying out of controversy? Was I hiding behind my job?

I recalled how close I'd come to joining the ROTC at Notre Dame. We had just arrived at South Bend—green with freshmanitis. And George had said, "What are you doin' that for? It's not compulsory." I can still see the sergeant playing an imaginary violin as I returned my uniform and walked out. To this day I wonder if George O'Donnell is the reason I got a two-year head start on a whole lot of potential talk-show hosts.

Whatever its cause, I was suffering near-terminal conflict. Whenever I had experienced inner conflict in the past, I had always turned to my faith and the Church. At Notre Dame I had attended Mass three or four times a week, and made many after-dinner visits to the Grotto of Our Lady—always prayers of supplication and thanksgiving, always a peaceful inner feeling, a comfort about really *believing* that not only were God and His Mother listening to me: I was also privileged to have been born a member of the One True Church and probably destined thereby to achieve Salvation. At the Grotto I would bow my head and silently recite the "Memorare":

> Remember, O Most Gracious Virgin Mary
> That never was it known
> That anyone who fled to thy protection

> Implored thy help
> Or sought thy intercession
> Was left unaided . . .

This prayer asked the Virgin to petition Her Son for whatever favor was important at that time.

At 32, I turned again to my faith and my Church. But this time there was no peace, no Grotto, no comfort. Instead, there was a church filled with people who were on Automatic as they walked into and out of Mass, a paternalistic church that had placed cardboard boxes in the vestibule for the collection of canned goods and old clothes for the St. Vincent De Paul Society. Incarnation Church conducted a monthly raffle to help raise money for the "temporal needs" of the parish. Suddenly I realized that very few people in the congregation were buying any raffle tickets. The chances were being sold to black people on Dayton's West Side, in the same way that the numbers game was flourishing in neighborhoods where welfare mothers weren't sure where their next meal was coming from. The American Catholic Church, which gave you bingo, was now, in Centerville, Ohio, bringing in thousands of dollars a year by selling chances to semi-educated poor people who were "prayin' that Jesus gonna take care of everything by bringin' home that winnin' raffle ticket." I was almost ready for Phase Three.

Before our voluntary busing program began, I had gone downtown to St. James, the predominantly black Catholic school that was to receive the white kids from the suburbs. I found a building in disrepair —leaky pipes in the boys' lavatory and textbooks dated 1953, with Cardinal Spellman's imprimatur ensuring that there was no information inside contrary to Catholic doctrine. The history books at St. James spoke of the missionaries who had come to America to "convert" the pagan Indians.

It was Catch-22. I was sending my kids to a predominantly black inner-city school (for a while, my son Michael and Dianne Fisher were the only white kids in their class) so that they wouldn't grow up with the same stereotypes that had been imposed on their father—that blacks either collected garbage or ran the hundred in 9.5 seconds. I wanted them to see black kids as kids, as people. That was the whole idea. But in their inner-city school they were taught the same old racist things I was trying to escape—while out in Centerville, at well-financed Incarnation school, the history books talked of Martin Luther

King and pictured him as well. The irony—suburban Incarnation offered schoolbooks with positive black images, while inner-city St. James passed out texts that featured minorities as the white man's burden!

More anger, more meetings, more beer and more rhetoric. The Fishers, the Breslins, the Swifts and the Donahues now had their Catholic speech:

> The Catholic Church's problem is not money [we said] but the manner by which it distributes the money it has. If the Catholic Church is going to continue the business of education, then it must see that *all* of its schools are *equally* supported. It is shameful [we said] that Incarnation has rugs on the floor, modern textbooks and overhead projectors while St. James is limping along on a shoestring. Whether or not your child gets a good Catholic education should not depend on the kind of neighborhood in which the school is located.

Our group of dissidents decided to take its message to the bishop personally. I bowed out of the summit conference for fear my celebrity status might distract His Grace from the issues of the meeting. I may have been flattering myself, but I was growing increasingly concerned that my public face might be getting in the way. Several people had accused me of trying to hype my show's ratings by creating a public Church fuss.

So down to Cincinnati went the dissidents. There in the office of the chancery seven people met face to face with a real live bishop, a person most Catholics see only during Confirmations and televised funerals. The group had all come through the Catholic ranks—adults in their 30s who had made their first Holy Communion, received a mother-of-pearl prayer book (black for boys, white for girls, with an inset crucifix), contributed to scores of "spiritual bouquets" for Mother's Day and Father's Day and marched in many May processions.

> "O Mary, we crown Thee
> With blossoms today—
> Queen of the angels,
> Queen of the May . . ."

In the month of May the women, as children, had even crowned the Virgin Mother's statue with a floral headpiece. These were born-once

Catholics who *knew* they were Catholics for life. All of them who gathered that day in the office of His Grace Edward A. McCarthy, auxiliary bishop of the Archdiocese of Cincinnati, were sincerely committed and devout Catholics. They were Catholics who, as children, had spent an "hour with Jesus" at 3 o'clock in the morning during the "Perpetual Adoration" liturgy known as Forty Hours. They had also given up candy for Lent and attended Sorrowful Mother novenas during which penitent Catholics bowed their heads and asked God to allow them, with the crucified Christ, to suffer: "More to suffer my God, ah, more."

Bishop McCarthy listened to them patiently as they made their pitch: Catholic-school integration is necessary now. To do otherwise is to ignore Christ's teaching. Further, because the Catholic Church is in the education business, it is obliged to provide an equally funded education for all its pupils, regardless of race. They told him about the maintenance problems at St. James and the need for money to refurbish the school building and to purchase new textbooks. They talked about the lack of equipment and how wrong it was that suburban schools got so much while inner-city schools got so little; why Centerville needed a million-dollar church.

When the Centervillians concluded their case, the Bishop politely thanked them for their concern and in a way not at all consistent with the stereotype of the pompous ecclesiastic, promised to examine the issues they had raised and assured them of a full report following his study of the Incarnation Church controversy. He also reminded the petitioners that the Archdiocese of Cincinnati was funding St. James Church with $25,000 per year.

Then His Grace, the Auxiliary Bishop and Vicar General of the Archdiocese of Cincinnati, shifted slightly in his chair and delivered a line that will forever ring in the minds of Catholic do-gooders who know the frustration of banging head on into the side of the barnacled Church bureaucracy. It is a line which, by itself, embodies all the paternalism, condescension and arrogance that so often mark the behavior of the men in power in the Church. It is also a clarion call for inaction.

The bishop looked at the group and said, "The poor we will always have with us."

The poor we will always have with us! The parishioners, who had prepared thoroughly for the meeting, left empty-handed. Furious, they returned to the Breslins' family room—and more beer, and more shouting of strategy and, finally, an agreement that we could no longer "go through channels." We unanimously decided to do something no one in our group had ever dreamed of: we decided we were going to picket the Bishop's office and his cathedral in Cincinnati.

Our strategy sessions became louder and more revolutionary. One of the meetings ended with a mock celebration of the Mass—with Jim Breslin playing the priest, draped in an old throw rug. (The rest of the "revolutionaries" served, and the "Mass" concluded to the tune of war whoops and convulsed laughter.) We were Catholics rebelling against a lifetime of boring liturgy and moral absolutes. We were granting ourselves a license for sacrilege. We were symbolically looking the bishop in the eye and giving him the finger. And we were drinking a lot of beer.

The decision to picket the chancery in Cincinnati confronted me with another moral dilemma. The company I worked for, Avco Broadcasting, was headquartered in Cincinnati. Avco's president was a highly visible Cincinnati Catholic named John T. Murphy. President Murphy was very much connected to the Cincinnati Catholic establishment, a fact confirmed by several wall plaques in his office. His company owned WLW-T in Cincinnati, as well as the sister station I worked for, WLW-D in Dayton. My show had recently premiered, and while it was doing fairly well, I was convinced he would be capable of firing me for embarrassing the one true Church. Just what "Mr. Insecure" needed: another moral dilemma.

I had ducked Matt Thompson; could I duck this too? After much agonizing, I decided I had no choice but to take part in the demonstration, and on a clear Sunday morning several station wagons, filled with adults, children and cardboard signs, made their way down Interstate 75 from Dayton to Cincinnati.

We arrived at St. Peter in Chains ("More to suffer, my God, ah, more") Cathedral during one of the Masses, assembled on the sidewalk outside, grasped our signs and began a slow march around the church building. My heart pounded. Our signs read CATHOLIC SCHOOLS UNFAIR and CATHOLIC SCHOOLS INTEGRATE NOW. Presently a white car with a telephone aerial on the back pulled around the corner. I noticed the lettering on the side of the vehicle: ACTION NEWS WLW-T CHANNEL 5. My mouth went dry.

Two news reporters got out, and one, with a camera, stationed himself on the sidewalk, focused on the line of marchers and started filming. As I got closer and closer to the camera, my sign got closer and closer to my face. And as I marched past the camera, all that showed was four disembodied limbs and a sign reading, DON'T AGI-

19. Ron Weiner directing on the Mississippi—December 1977.

20. Warming up the audience at Madison Square Garden's Felt Forum during a remote—New York City, May 1979.

21. "The Star" arrives at work, wardrobe in hand.

22. Showing off for photographers at the Emmy Awards presentation—New York City, May 17, 1979.

23. Pat McMillen, Producer of *Donahue*, and Richard Mincer, Executive Producer, accepting their first national Emmy Awards — New York City, June 7, 1978.

24. Later that evening—the staff celebrating our Emmys in a hotel room in Charleston, West Virginia, where we were taping a remote week. I had to fly to Chicago that night for a speech. Left to right: Deanne Mincer, Penny Rotheiser, Dick Mincer, Pat McMillen, Ron Weiner, Sheri Singer, Darlene Hayes.

25. With Henry Winkler and softball fans after a game between the *Happy Days* cast and the Chicago Media All-Stars at Wrigley Field—Chicago, August 17, 1979.

26. Softball practice with the WGN "729ers"—I can throw my glove like Lou Boudreau, but I can't "hit. . . ."

27. Christmas in Aspen—1978. Left to right: Dennis O'Connell, Mike, Marlo, me, Susan O'Connell, Mary Rose, Dan, Kevin, Jim.

28. In Hawaii with our "founder," Don Dahlman, Executive Vice-President–Sales for Multimedia Program Productions, Inc.; Marlo; and Babs Dahlman—May 1978.

29, 30. Laughs with Marlo in
Rome—summer, 1978.

31. With Mary Rose during one of our winter vacations.

32. With Marlo at a black-tie fund-raiser—Dayton, 1978.

33. Interviewing Norman Lear on the *Donahue on Today* set at WMAQ-TV—Chicago, June 13, 1979.

34. With the newest members of the *Donahue* staff—Chicago, October 1979. Back row, left to right: Denise Lanton, Joycelyn Marnul, Lillian Smith, "the boss," Cynthia Patrasso, Wendy Roth. Front row, left to right: Joe DiCanio, Marilyn O'Reilly, Lillian Handler, Dorothy Foster Ghallab.

TATE, INTEGRATE. I felt like a nominee for Coward of the Year. The demonstration ended with the departure of the newsmen, and we returned to Dayton.

Well, I thought, I had finally done it. I had taken a risk and banged up against a system that had, for my entire life, provided all the answers. For the first time in my life, I had said that I did not accept those answers. And I had said it publicly. If my grandmother had been alive, she would have been very worried that I was losing my faith.

The busing program, meanwhile, was under way, with eleven white families and thirteen black families. Some of the blacks were bused to Incarnation while the Donahue kids were making the trip downtown. Of all the parents who took part in the "Voluntary Exchange Program," none was as dedicated as Curtis Niles, a black man who kept his faith, his pride, his love and his anger in meaningful focus at all times. He had become our moral leader, and when I first noticed the growth on his neck I was not alarmed. When I went to visit him at the Dayton VA hospital, I could not believe he was dying. In a small room with pale green walls (and no window curtains), his body convulsed as it took in breath so irregularly that I was certain at several times that he had died. He died the next day, and when three white and three black pallbearers carried his body into St. James Church, Bishop McCarthy said the Requiem Mass.

The gatherings of the busing parents continued and kept us in touch with each other, but except for these planned teas, there was disappointingly little social interaction between the black parents and the white parents. Occasionally black chums from Michael's class would sleep over. Two frequent visitors were the Dickens twins. Neighbors stared out their windows when the twins played ball in our backyard. All in all, it was a small-scale effort, and it wasn't very well organized, but we thought it was a beginning of the effort to stop Catholics from "raising another generation of racists."

The Dickens twins' mother was an attractive schoolteacher; their father, Charles, a tall, athletic man who, when he wasn't coaching his sons in sports, worked at the Dayton airport as a skycap. Dickens and I had spent our share of time together at busing meetings and visiting St. James School. Thus, every trip I made through the Dayton airport was an occasion for terror. I had a frightful anxiety that one day I would pull up in front of the TWA entrance and the only skycap in sight would be Charles Dickens. Charles Dickens was a friend, and he was black. My nightmare had him grabbing my bags and me obliged to tip him. How much? Would he expect it? Would he be embarrassed? Is this really a problem or am I creating one? Please, God, don't let Charles Dickens carry my bags! In the scores of times I arrived at the Dayton airport, loaded down with luggage for a week of far-flung telecasts, I never once encountered Charles Dickens. And I can still feel the relief.

By then the busers were notorious. Busing in Centerville was a little like flashing in Centerville. Two men visited me once in near panic. They had heard that I was going to sell our house to a black family. They said they "knew it was coming, but we didn't expect it this soon." I assured them I had no intention of selling the house to anyone and they left relieved, but still anxious.

One night around midnight, as I lay in bed unable to sleep because of the August heat and stifling humidity, a car pulled up outside. It was filled with young people. A male teen-ager yelled, "Donahue eats nigger shit."

I had entered Phase Three.

Phase Three is a sudden, overwhelming realization of the awesome magnitude of the problem. It is a depressing awareness that all your meetings and all the rhetoric and all the excitement about "making progress" is a self-delusion. Phase Three liberals have finally realized that racism is woven into the fabric of American society and we will not see it raveled out in our lifetime. For me, the fun of organizing Camp Dakota was over, the anger at parishioners who didn't care what the church building cost just so it was "nice" was also gone. I was suddenly alone—not happy, not angry, just alone. For me, Phase Three was the bitter disappointment of realizing that very, very few people were going to follow our lead and voluntarily bus their children, that the Church of the Incarnation was going to be built at the cost of $1 million, that Catholics were still going to mindlessly support the Vietnam war and that the bishops were going to continue to tell their flock that "the poor we will always have with us." Phase Three was best expressed by one of our disenchanted group after a night of strategy planning, beer drinking and mock-liturgical revelry: we had gotten "goddamn nowhere."

Phase Three people meditate. For me, it was discovering that the Church not only was racist and sexist: it was a lot of other things. Now my mind was racing. The questions began to surface like Old Faithful. For the first time in my life I was asking all those questions which had been so effectively repressed during all those high school

Theology classes, all those Christian Family Movement meetings and all those weekend retreats:

● Why do babies, who do not ask to be born, enter the world with the stain of "original sin"?

● How could an all-knowing, all-loving God allow His Son to be murdered on a cross in order to redeem my sins?

● If God the Father is so "all-loving," why didn't *He* come down and go to Calvary? Then Jesus could have said, "This is my Father, in whom *I* am well pleased."

● If there is life on other planets, do those people need salvation too?

● If sex is so beautiful, why did God circumvent it to bring His "only begotten" Son into the world?

● If mass murderers occasionally get a parole review, how come Hell is not appealable? Is God less forgiving than we are?

● And if there is no Hell, then why do we need the crucifixion? From what are we being redeemed?

● Why is the Holy Roman Catholic Church so insecure about the loyalty of its members that it imposes everlasting damnation on those who choose to leave?

Conclusion: The Church is not irrelevant; it is destructive. It is unnecessarily destructive. It is a hurdle not worthy of my energy. It is retarding growth, inhibiting my ability to reach out. I am 34 years old, and something has happened to me that I had been warned about—a warning that came from the nuns, and the priests in the confessional. My house of cards had collapsed. I had lost my faith.

Enter Phase Four.

Phase Four is where the saints are made. It is where the liberal finally comes face to face with unfiltered reality. Phase Four people go one of two ways. Either they stay in there swinging, despite the knowledge of their powerlessness, or they go the way of yoga, guitar lessons, astrology, psychiatry or just plain unglamorous, uncamouflaged dropping out.

The "saints" adapt to the absence of the big dramatic breakthroughs. They no longer expect goose bumps when torchlight marchers sing "We Shall Overcome." The oratory has long since faded. There are no banquets honoring anybody, no thunderous applause, no gratitude, no headline victories. There are just inches—scratching at the problem, sweating, progress measured in inches. Saints know that at every turn there are people in power patting them on the head saying, "The poor we will always have with us"—and they keep trying anyway. The "saints" are Matt Thompson and Curtis Niles and countless other people who have seen the world as it is, and who recognize the "awesome enormity" of the problem, and who nevertheless continue in the struggle, with a lot of love and only a little anger.

I am neither a saint nor a guitar player. I am a person whose professional life has taken some very dramatic and very time-consuming turns. I am no longer charging out to open-house meetings, no longer lining up buses for integrated summer camps, no longer picketing anything. The waves I make are made on my program, and I get a lot of attention for that. And the money's good. I am a Phase Four person with a lot to think about. The big guilt is gone, the laughter is a little freer now, the anger has diminished, but the commitment is beige. I am not suffering, but I am not at peace either.

On June 6, 1969, the Church of the Incarnation was dedicated with all the pomp and holy water befitting a brand-new house of the Lord. The building was definitely in keeping with the neighborhood. It cost over $1 million, and it has central air conditioning. It is, most of the time, empty and dark.

Of the four couples who originally gathered to challenge the decision to build that church, two are divorced, one has moved to the country with an unlisted phone and none, repeat none, goes to church. Any church.

The Phil Donahue Show

November 6, 1967, at 10:30 a.m. EST, I introduced my first guest on my first TV program to a Dayton audience. The guest was Madalyn Murray O'Hair, the atheist.

There were other "guests" at the program that day—ticket holders for *The Johnny Gilbert Show*. They had come to see the good-looking Gilbert and to hear him sing, and maybe to win a prize. Instead they were treated to insults by a woman who not only did not believe in God but had worked to throw prayer out of the public schools—and who suggested that religion "breeds dependence" and makes it impossible for "Christians to stand on their own two feet."

It was like calling for a return of polio.

Our second show featured single men talking about what they looked for in women and what on earth in 1967 were nice-looking guys like them doing single? Not exactly *60 Minutes*, but a welcome relief from our opener with Mrs. Attila the Hun.

Wednesday of premiere week featured a Dayton obstetrician and a film of the birth of a baby; Thursday, a funeral director (I actually reclined inside the coffin. "The mourners should not have to *look in* the casket; the body should be visible above the rim," he said) and Friday, a promoter pushing the "Little Brother" doll, an anatomically correct male doll, which I solemnly held up to the cameras sans diaper. I asked viewers to vote on whether "this toy is objectionable for children. Vote *yes* by dialing BA 1-2693; vote *no* by dialing BA 1-6842." The entire Baldwin exchange, serving all of downtown Dayton, was tied up by the overload of calls. Hundreds of other calls were interrupted, hospital switchboards went out and in the panic that followed, Ohio Bell finally rushed a man to our studio to plead for an end to the poll.

It was a helluva first week. Sharing it with me were two other people, Dick Mincer, producer-director, and Patricia McMillen, secretary, both of whom I had inherited from Channel 2. ("If you don't like them, we'll get somebody else.") We worked out of an "office" that had once served as a wrestler's dressing room. The three of us had no idea, that first boffo week, that we had embarked on an adventure that would take all of us from Dayton, Ohio—home of NCR, Frigidaire, Pneumatic Tool and Foundry Supply and BHA—into every state in the Union and into the lives of millions of people. We also had no idea that during the next decade we would spend considerable time and energy explaining to the men who manage America's television stations just what it was we did ("No band?") and why a program that broke so many rules ("Just one guest?") appealed to so many women.

There was no way for any of us to know what was coming. In fact, I wasn't sure at all, during that week of November 6, 1967, what was already here. My well-nourished Irish Catholic anxiety about succeeding at anything had me hoping and praying for a successful local show, which, in spite of graphic portrayals of life and death during the first week of programs, was anything but assured. I suffered near-terminal gloom at just the thought of our show, featuring one talking head without benefit of orchestra, competing against Monty Hall, who was on the other channel presenting a $5,000 check to a woman dressed like a chicken-salad sandwich.

On January 4, 1968, two months after our premiere program, my father died. Years of selling (and "shlepping") furniture and a lifelong cigarette habit brought him down in his 64th year. It was his second heart attack. My father had been one of twelve children, and had spent his 20's trying to survive as a musician in the teeth of the depression.

Although he did not finish high school, he was bright, had the most beautiful handwriting I have ever seen by a man and could, in the words of the furniture men in northern Ohio who knew him, "sell a dead rat."

My father was kind and loving and seemed to worry excessively about the physical well-being of his two children. He raised his voice in anger at me only once, and that was the night he caught me riding my bicycle in the street without a light.

When he died in Fairview Hospital in suburban Cleveland, *The Phil Donahue Show* had presented only about forty shows, and they were seen only in Dayton. He knew about the program, and I know he was proud it bore his name. But he never saw it. And I will always feel the sadness of that.

It may have been a full three years before any of us began to understand that our program was something special. The show's style had developed not by genius but by necessity. The familiar talk-show heads were not available to us in Dayton, Ohio. Although we were able to attract a Phyllis Diller or a Paul Lynde during the summer months when the "Hollywood stars" worked the Kenley Theatre circuit in Ohio, after the biggies left town we were left with a lot of open dates to fill. The result was improvisation.

For example: a woman whose daughter was on a protest fast in the Greene County Jail calling for an end to the Vietnam war.

AUDIENCE: "What if she dies?"

MOTHER: "If she dies, she dies."

AUDIENCE: "You have an obligation to her."

MOTHER: "You have an obligation to the men coming home dead from this war."

After two years as a local program, *The Phil Donahue Show* was picked up by other Avco stations, and Don Dahlman was on the road looking for additional markets.

Slowly, very slowly, the program was taking hold in Dayton, Columbus, Cincinnati, Cleveland, Detroit and several other Midwest cities. Slowly, very slowly, women at home during the day were discovering us. Mincer, McMillen and I were improvising, not because we wanted to, but because we *had* to. Phyllis Diller had gone home. Whatever else they said about us, the result was a show that was different from anything else on the air. And more and more women were writing for tickets, and when they finally got them (and the baby-sitter, and their husband's breakfast), they rolled down I-75 to our studios, and when they took their seats in our audience and the red camera lights went on, they stood and said what they had to say.

And they were *smart*. And the sponsors—no dummies themselves—were saying, "Where in hell does he get those women?" And almost by accident, we were off. . . .

In that first, nerve-racking week of *The Phil Donahue Show*, Dick, Pat and I wondered only if we were good enough to succeed locally. Twleve years later, *Donahue* would air in 200 markets including Alaska, Hawaii and Puerto Rico, and Dick, Pat and I would receive Emmys for "Best Host" and "Best Show" and we would know that we had the best daily hour on television. We would move into the number one position in America's syndicated-talk-show derby, and the three people who began the race in a cold sweat from a wrestler's dressing room in Dayton would wonder why it had taken us so long to get there.

And I would reckon the cost.

9
Dayton to Chicago

WHEN I was a kid, people who got divorced were people who had no gumption. "Gumption" was a favorite word of the adults in my childhood world. It was easier to say than "stick-to-it-iveness," and meant a little more. Kids who cut the lawn without being told had gumption. So did kids who walked right up to Joe DiMaggio at Cleveland Stadium after a game to ask for an autograph. If the Jews had chutzpah, the Catholics had gumption. Unless they got divorced.

Catholics who got divorced were people who didn't try hard enough. In the eyes of the Church, divorcing two practicing Catholics was like surgically separating Siamese twins—and having them both die! These people were definitely "sundered"—something no man should do to two people whom God had joined together. I never worried about divorce because I knew it was an option that would never be open to me.

That made getting married not more difficult, but easier. Having solved the problem of divorce by not even considering it a possibility, I had walked down the aisle to make a life commitment without trauma or doubt. Besides, for all my insecurity, my reservations about myself and my uncertain future, I knew when I gave Margaret M. Cooney of Albuquerque, New Mexico, a diamond ring, that This Was It, because there was no changing the marriage contract. It was a case of reverse logic. I started with the conclusion that marriage was a binding commitment and worked backward from that. From my conclusion I developed my hypothesis. If marriage is forever, then what I was doing in that year 1958 in San Felipe de Neri Church in the Old Town section of Albuquerque was "logically" and without question *forever* and ever, Amen.

We were married in one of the oldest churches in North America, kneeling on an altar with three priests (Solemn High Nuptial Mass), lots of servers and lots of flowers. It was a perfect ceremony and a perfect day. After the Mass and a reception at the Alvarado Hotel, my father-in-law told my bride in a stage whisper that "there'll be a strange man in your room when you awake in the morning," and we departed for Bishop's Lodge in Santa Fe, where I would finally, and without guilt, lose my virginity!

Pregnancy and parenthood were guaranteed military deferments, and my number was coming up at the local draft board; we waited an eternity of four months. Michael was born two days before our first anniversary, January 30, 1959, several weeks premature and weighing four pounds. On December 9, 1959, Kevin was born, also several weeks premature and weighing four pounds. Both spent several days in an Isolette and came home weighing five pounds, and both, for God's sake, were born in the *same year!*

When we had been married six years we had five children. Much later I would realize how ill prepared I was for fatherhood. My energy had been directed toward achieving at WHIO. Fatherhood, I thought, was a natural responsibility that required no training and could be discharged in the evenings. Later I would look back appalled at the enormous failure of my education. I had never been told that children *needed* to be cuddled, *needed* approval and attention, *needed* measured and thoughtful discipline. I honestly thought that being a father meant giving presents at Christmas and birthdays, occasionally changing diapers, occasionally spanking and occasionally baby-sitting for "the little woman's night out." Besides, the emphasis on pre-Cana (Catholic-ese for marriage-preparation) classes at Notre Dame had been on "finding a good woman"—translated: get a nurturing, patient, loving, long-suffering wife, and you have just about solved the marriage problem.

When, at age 39, I became legally and spiritually "sundered," I thought of my professional ambition and how costly it had been to my family. I thought of how I had been married to my job instead of my wife. I thought about the time I had listened to Lou Emm in the labor room while Margie struggled with labor pains and waited for some attention from her husband, who had a radio pressed against his ear. I wondered, at age 39, how many other males of the fifties had likewise sleepwalked into (and sometimes through) parenthood and marriage.

I thought about the early years, after the wedding, and what an insensitive and lousy lover I had been. I thought about the number of times I had bragged about having five children without realizing it took no talent at all. I thought about the cultural cover-ups for workaholism: "Oh, Dad, poor Dad, he works so hard!" And I began to understand that in far too many homes, "poor Dad" was not coming home till 8 o'clock at night because he didn't want to. He was after a lifetime of steady Horatio Alger, conditioned to be more challenged at work than he was at home. The consequences on the kids and the wives, and not surprisingly on the men themselves, were incalculable!

By now Margie's unhappiness was so apparent that even I had noticed it. I was suddenly dealing with the very real possibility that she would leave me and take the kids with her. The unthinkable, the scenario that was not even a *possibility* at the time of our marriage, was actually taking place. Death was not parting us—Margie's unhappiness was. And I still couldn't believe it.

I thought about my childhood and my education and how nothing, absolutely nothing, was ever said about human relationships, and introspection, and mood swings, and listening, and sending flowers for no reason at all. I thought about how on guard we were against "bad thoughts," and I wondered if all of us who came out of the forties and fifties weren't just a little crippled by the emphasis on sexual sins. Is it any wonder that for millions of men the only intimacy is physical, and silent, and predictable? Did our parents' fear of adolescent sex (reinforced as it was by the teachings of the Church) cause an overkill that left all of us (the boys especially) mortally wounded in other areas of intimacy? Has it left generations of men totally incapable of verbalizing a fear, sharing a cry or squeezing a hand? How did we become so blocked? Why are so many men gathered in taverns and bars drinking beer and discussing football teams while their women, who fought them off during the courtship, sit at home wondering what happened to all that premarital gusto?

I thought about the pain of our last married years—the terrible fear of not seeing my children grow up, the near-panic at the thought of being alone. I even had gone to a psychiatrist to find out what was wrong with me! I hadn't fooled around, I hadn't been violent, I hadn't blown my paychecks. What, on God's earth, was wrong with me? I recalled the long, uncomfortable wait in the shrink's office, deathly afraid of being recognized, and how, when I finally got inside, I did what I do best. I talked. In fact, I threw up a torrent of words. "I don't care what it takes," I said. "Do whatever you have to. I want to save my marriage! Put me through the meat grinder!" And how the psychiatrist had leaned forward, offered me a Kleenex and, stroking his beard as in a bad movie, said, "There is no meat grinder."

In the summer of 1973 Margie and I separated. She rented an apartment in Albuquerque and lived there with two of the children, while I awkwardly began the job of playing the role of both parents to the remaining three kids—no small job.

In Centerville, I did the best I could explaining to the neighbors what had happened, preparing meals (barbecued steaks on Monday night, TV dinners on Tuesday), learning how the washing machine works, getting to work on time and all the while "auditioning" women who were to become very important in my life. They were called "housekeepers," and whatever their virtues, they were also to provide some of my biggest problems.

One absolutely perfect applicant for the job—a good cook, strong references—was introduced to the children, agreed to the salary terms and then at the appointed hour—failed to show up. I never heard from her again.

After ten months, and scores of TV dinners, Margie and her hassled husband decided to try a reconciliation. At the same time this personal decision was being made, a very big professional decision was being made as well. *The Phil Donahue Show* was moving to Chicago. The decision to move our act to a bigger town followed six years of trying to encourage program guests to come to Dayton. The growth of our show had stalled at about thirty-eight cities, and it became clear that *Donahue* in Dayton had gone about as far as it was going to go.

After a frantic search, I purchased a three-story, six-bedroom house in Kenilworth (a North Shore community that boasted the highest per capita income in the Greater Chicago area), and the reunited Donahue family settled in.

The reconciliation failed.

Four months later, Margie left with *all the kids* for Albuquerque and I began the longest six months of my life. There is nothing emptier than a house once occupied by a wife and five children, unless it is a king-size bed once occupied by two people. For me, every day alone in Kenilworth was like not having a date on New Year's Eve. I was up at 4:30 almost every day. At 5, I would be jogging down Essex Avenue, past the Kenilworth Presbyterian Church and large, stately mansions and raccoons sitting curiously in the middle of the street—

then back to a house that seemed even emptier than before. I thought about all the divorced fathers everywhere and wondered if they were in as much pain as I was.

When, later that year, I obtained custody of the four boys (under a voluntary agreement) I was quite literally reborn! I had sold the Kenilworth house, by then referred to as "the Mausoleum," and rented a house in Winnetka, where I enrolled Jim, then 12, in the neighborhood school and the other three boys in New Trier High School. I missed Mary Rose terribly, but her frequent phone calls kept us "together." She had been accepted in Youth Orchestra as a violinist, and I was very proud. Mary Rose has understood her father's longing for his only daughter and in a most mature and loving way tries to relieve my unhappiness by saying all the right things. She is now 14 and has the insight of a very caring fully grown adult. In the simplest terms, she can be identified as "a great kid." I was counting my blessings.

I was also counting socks! For a while I was convinced that parenthood equaled socks. I couldn't believe how many there were and how dirty they looked. Not just tattletale gray—they were black. In fact, I was beginning to notice a lot of things that had never caught my attention before—like other people's floors. Without knowing it, I was slowly being absorbed into a whole new life experience. It is called motherhood.

At the laundromat I would be caught with two full washing machines and no change, staggered by the number of coin boxes and coin combinations they took. The washing machines took 60 cents—two quarters and a dime or two nickels, but not one quarter, three dimes and a nickel, or six dimes, or twelve nickels. The dryers took two dimes for six minutes, not a quarter (keep the nickel) or four nickels! The soap dispenser took 15 cents, but only in the form of one dime and one nickel. And I had to hover as the spin cycle ended for fear an angry fellow customer would empty my machine with less concern for the contents than I had. And all the while I am trying to look comfortable (and praying that I will not be recognized) by pretending to read an old magazine in the glare of fluorescent light.

Soon I began getting my act together. I acquired a washer and dryer of my own, and not only did it run without coins: I didn't have to be there when the spin cycle ended. And I could do my wash without wearing a hat to hide my face. And I soon became a very sophisticated domestic: the Downy goes in the rinse cycle.

My effort to find the one true, perfect housekeeper continued, and so did my frustration. (There is no real "Aunt Bea.")

Housekeepers come in all sizes, ages, colors and shapes. They also come with a full bag of "shoulds." "Jim should eat his vegetables." "Danny should wash his hair." One housekeeper served squid with the eyes staring up; another wept because Jim wouldn't eat anything green. But almost all of them liked me—not because of any inordinate homemaking talent of mine, but precisely because of the lack of it. There's nothing quite so attractive to some women as a father trying to raise his kids and being inept at it.

I thought about all the women in America who were raising children alone, without benefit of live-in help and without benefit of my income, and I realized one more feature of the culture's double standard. Women in my circumstances are expected to raise children *and* money, without applause. When men do it, they are showered with attention and admiration, and if they're lousy at it, they take on the "little boy lost" aura, which makes them even more attractive. When I think of the countless women in this country who get up in the morning, make breakfast, see that the kids are dressed properly, send them off to school, dress, go to work, come home, make dinner, speak to the emotional needs of the children, do the wash, retire and get up again in the morning only to do it all over again, I don't know how the hell they do it! My fantasies about "my four sons" have been lowered, and my consciousness raised.

As each week passed, I began to feel better about my situation. I finally found the help I needed in a loving, hard-working Yugoslavian couple and I began to sleep past 4:30 in the morning. In 1976 I purchased a new five-bedroom house in Winnetka with a special apartment for the help. Above all, I retrieved one of my most important emotional requirements, one that I had enjoyed for sixteen years of marriage but always took for granted—noise in the house.

The kids meanwhile have settled down. Michael and Kevin each have a car and an after-school job. Dan is finally using Borax on his hands after work at a gas station. At New Trier, he was reading *Ethan Frome* in his sophomore year and hating every word of it. He would rather be under the hood of a car, and was—at the Union 76—every day after school. He was earning $2.50 an hour and totally absorbed in his job, if not in *Ethan Frome,* which he was flunking. He was only 14 and had lied about his age to get the job.

I began to wonder why New Trier was force-feeding *Ethan Frome* to a teen-age car junkie and also became curious about a society that forces a 14-year-old to lie in order to work. We constantly tell teen-agers to be responsible and then give them nothing but *Ethan Frome* (and maybe Ohm's law) to be responsible about. I was determined to pressure all the boys to work—thus avoiding the "TV stare" and the slumped-over body surrounded by empty Coke cans. My message was clear: bored kids are lazy kids are (sometimes) antisocial kids.

Michael and Kevin, working at an A&P for a little more than $3 an hour, wanted to know why they had to join the retail clerks' union. The initiation fee was $107 and the weekly dues were $11. They couldn't understand why a student part-timer has to pay full-time dues, and who needs all this union junk mail anyway? Pamphlets were arriving at the house extolling the wonderful breakthroughs of the retail clerks' union, offering case histories of union grievance victories, and the Donahues were spending most of dinnertime arguing the right-to-work issue.

Their consciousness was growing, along with their bank accounts, although the latter much more slowly. My deal with the boys was that as long as they worked they did not have to do routine chores around the house. The boys bought the whole package. I have learned that my kids, like most kids, would rather work all night long in a salt mine than rake leaves at home. I hired a gardener.

Jim got into music with guitar lessons. He was determined, and I liked the way he used his time. He was 13 and got a pass on finding a job.

I was becoming a little more comfortable as a single parent in a strong nuclear-family community. I connected socially with Dennis and Susan O'Connell, who, with their two small children, were my only source of local social activity. We got along fine, and they seemed not uncomfortable when we traveled to the movies and the symphony in threes. I had learned to be a semicomfortable sit-on-the-porch-and-drink-a-beer North Shore resident.

I had also learned some other things about the North Shore of greater Chicago, and so had my kids.

Jim said a boy at school became angry at him during gym and called him a "dirty Jew." He wanted to know why that was an insult. When I first moved into our third home on the fabled North Shore, the first area resident to welcome me explained that my next-door neighbors "are Jewish, *but* very nice."

Earlier, when I sold my house in Kenilworth (a community with a Chicago-wide reputation of being very WASP-ish and very closed), my real estate woman, after a Sunday open house, said the only action had been a "Cadillac that passed by driven by a big fat Jew."

While I had been exposed to anti-Jewish remarks before, I had never heard comments like this so often and in such a relatively small area. Just when I thought I might be drawing too many negative conclusions, another resident offered (without my asking) that he didn't have anything against Jewish neighbors, he just wished "there weren't so many of them moving to the North Shore."

"All of western Wilmett is *gone*," he said. Make that *Jewish*.

The Donahue boys believed that there were three cops in Winnetka for every teen-ager. They suddenly found themselves arrested for everything: running a stop sign, driving without a Winnetka sticker, hitchhiking, speeding and almost every moving violation in the book. It was clear that in Winnetka, The Book is a mighty detailed one and that the cops are ready to throw it at a teen-ager at the drop of a gear. One cop arrested Danny for hitchhiking and searched his wallet. During a suspected pot bust, the cops lined the kids up against the car. It's as though North Shore cops feel a car full of teen-agers is a car full of dope. I have seen teen-agers stopped for a traffic violation in a busy Winnetka shopping area and while passersby look on, the girls' handbags are routinely searched (with the aid of flashlights) without regard for the U.S. Constitution or the dignity of the young people detained.

At dinner Mike, Kev, Dan and Jim wanted to know why the cops are so aggressive, and I said something about "conservative" and "property" and a high tax base and "attitudes." I tried to explain that some people have small children and for them there still aren't enough cops, stop signs and traffic lights. Danny wanted to know if it was legal for a cop to search his wallet. I said, "Not without probable cause, but let's not make World War III out of it, because I'll look like the big-shot TV guy who thinks his kids are perfect." Danny shrugged and went back to his dinner and the moral question passed not totally answered.

The first two Winnetka winters came and went and we welcomed spring again. The North Shore was developed around the turn of the century, so the trees are very mature and very beautiful. Large, drooping tree branches overhang streets, cathedral-like, and when the last snows of Chicago's brutal winter pass, the smell along the North Shore is unmistakably spring.

While spring bursts forth along Chicago's fabled North Shore, so do the cops. Kevin was arrested for cutting through the A&P parking lot at midnight, I was stopped for turning right at a stop sign without using my directionals and Dennis O'Connell was arrested for riding his bicycle without a light.

COP: "How old are you?"
DENNIS: "Thirty-four."

Dennis and I get a pass; Kevin gets a ticket, a court date and a $20 fine. Police motto: Winnetka would be a wonderful place to live if it didn't have teen-agers.

Slowly, very slowly, the boys and I were beginning to understand the "ways" of North Shore life. Just when I began to feel that the "freak father" and his four "outlaw sons" were being accepted in Chicago's northern suburbs, something happened downtown that was to provide the first evidence that maybe—just maybe—I was being accepted by Chicago.

It was an incident that more than anything else gave proof of Chicago citizenship. I was to actually meet, in person, Richard J. Daley.

Meeting Mayor Daley was to Chicago what baptism is to the Church. It happened at the annual municipal testimonial to the mayor called the St. Patrick's Day Parade. I was invited to march with the mayor as a "Son of Erin." I didn't realize it then, but being asked to march with the Sons of Erin was no small honor. When I arrived at State and Lake for the beginning of what was to be a four-hour stand-on-your-feet-and-look-pleased experience, I was surrounded by state judges, county judges, union bosses, ward bosses, would-be bosses and various kinds of hangers-on. Wearing a green ribbon across my leather overcoat, I made no attempt to meet "Da Mare," as columnist Mike Royko called him. I took a position well inside the pack and watched the green fedora bob up and down as His Honor, shillelagh in hand, led us the four blocks to the reviewing stand, where we all stood watching the bands and the floats pass by. Signs read GOD BLESS YOU MAYOR DALEY, PLUMBERS LOCAL 105. Small children were held high by large smiling men in VFW hats, and all the time "Da Mare," standing next to Chicago's John Cardinal Cody, smiled and waved his approval. Security personnel collected flowers offered to the man who was the most honored, respected and loved living human being I had ever seen with my own eyes. As I stood in the back of the reviewing stand, a strong hand grasped my arm and a man in a black overcoat wearing a green carnation motioned for me to step forward. I knew immediately that I had been chosen to actually *meet* Mayor Richard J. Daley, personally.

"Mayor, I want you to meet the new talk-show host at WGN . . . Phil Donahue. Phil, meet Mayor Daley . . ."

"How do you do, Mr. Mayor?"

"How do you do, Bill?"

10
Single

THERE IS no way in the world for a father of five children to describe the feeling of being introduced at age 39 as "my boyfriend." But that is how I was being identified by women who, for lack of a better word (and God, how I wish there were a better word), are called "*dates.*"

It had been seventeen years since I had had a "date," and the only thing that hadn't changed was my wing-tipped shoes. It was like being back in college with gray hair. It was a déjà vu nightmare in which all the old lines ("What's your major?") no longer worked. People who knew me would extend an arm for a "How-ya-been?" handshake while all the time staring at the woman next to me. The women next to me always seemed to be 24 years old, and I always seemed to be not so much shy as terrified.

I could not even *consider* going anywhere alone. The private clubs and the singles bars were beyond my emotional tolerance. I could not bear the possibility of being approached by a disco dandy in imitation Halston wearing Bal à Versailles perfume who might say, "What are *you* doing *here?*"

One woman I dated was a "flight attendant." (It was much easier for me to say I was "seeing" a flight attendant rather than a "stewardess.")

She was kind and smart and pretty and put the lie to all those "Coffee-tea-or-me?" stories. She also seemed interested in *me,* and not my celebrity status. Once, during a TV football party in her apartment, I stood around nervously trying to appear comfortable with the crowd of co-pilots and flight attendants. While in a conversation with one of the young women at the party I inquired about the identity of a particularly loud lampshade-on-the-head guy telling bad jokes in another corner of the room.

"Oh him," she said. "He's a retread."

"What's a retread?" I asked, knowing I looked dumb but unable to cope without the information.

"A retread is a divorced guy," she said.

Two of the women I "dated" were newspaper reporters who had come to the office to interview me. Talking about my background and cautiously sharing information about my marital status made it easier for me to suggest that we have "lunch sometime." I never opened with "dinner." "Lunch" had an innocent sound. "Dinner" sounded leering.

On only one occasion did I summon up enough courage to make a "cold call." She was a Chicago TV celebrity and although I had never met her personally, I knew she was single, and I knew from my nineteen-inch Sony that she was pretty. As I stammered through my invitation to a formal dinner (Mayor Daley was hosting the King of Sweden at the Conrad Hilton Ballroom), I felt as if I were back on Jane Halloran's front porch. She sounded surprised and I thought at least a little flattered, and when I knocked on her downtown apartment door (wearing my first completely owned, nonrented tuxedo) I was met by a woman who was even more beautiful in person, and by a Siamese cat who appeared to have no interest in me either as a private citizen or a famous television personality.

That evening I escorted my "date" to our assigned table and was very pleased to discover that our dinner companions were Sheriff and Mrs. Dick Elrod of Cook County and Mayor Daley's dentist—who, surprisingly, has only one arm. I had been in Chicago for two years and I was only just beginning to become part of the Semifraternal Chicago Order of Pecking, a complicated system of ego stroking that measures the value of a person by the identity of his dinner companions and the distance between his table and the center of the banquet, which was then invariably occupied by "Da Mare."

When "His Majesty, the King of Sweden, and Mayor Daley" were introduced and more than a thousand people stood in the Grand Ballroom of the Conrad Hilton Hotel, most of the guests looked on, applauding enthusiastically while this Odd Couple (Daley was 74, King Carl XVI Gustaf, 26) walked stiffly down the center aisle. But I knew that the majority of the Chicagoans there—mostly wealthy politicos with clout—had their eyes not on the King but on "Da King." After all, how much power did the King of Sweden have in Chicago?

Following the royal banquet, I walked my "date" to her door, and she invited me in "for coffee." Not a *leering* "drink," but *innocent* "coffee"—a big difference.

I nervously took off my coat, and as I sat down on her couch (at the opposite end from her Siamese cat) I suddenly heard a loud male voice. Just when I thought I had "seen this movie," I saw my "date" standing next to her automatic phone-answering machine. As I sat there being stared at by her cat, she listened to the entire evening's worth of phone calls, all from men and all asking for return calls. I drank a half a cup of coffee, put on my coat, kissed her chastely goodby, closed the front door, listened for the lock to snap on the inside and ran to my car.

That night en route home, I thought about all those fantasies of unhappily married men—about the Jack Lemmon type of guy in the high-rise with the Gucci loafers and the open shirt and the Italian horn. About the man who gets his divorce, buys a new stereo and a wine rack, and says, "Bring on the broads!"

And I thought about that damn Siamese cat.

And about being a retread.

In reality, the most important things happen when you don't look for them.

I had met her once before, in Dayton in 1972, when she was on the road promoting her TV special *Free to Be You and Me*. I remembered her as very bright, articulate, Catholic and sexy. She was a perfect Donahue guest—famous, beautiful, popular, very conversant with important issues like men and women, careers, role models, feminism, parenting and politics. And if all that didn't carry the show (which it did) we could always talk about her famous father. She was a "hangover guest"—the kind of guest I needed on those mornings when I felt headachy and not very sharp. I knew the moment I met her in the wrestler's dressing room in Dayton, Ohio, that here was a guest who would never, ever let me die on the air. She also had a great body, and if it had been 1953 she would have been a "bad thought."

The second time I met her was in Chicago, and a lot had happened to me in the interim. I was single, trying to raise four boys and just beginning to get used to the idea of being accompanied to social events by a woman who was not my wife. When I walked into our "greenroom" at WGN, her back was to me. When she turned, I immediately remembered the eyes, which hadn't changed since Dayton. Nor had the smile or the firm handshake.

Redbook had recorded a conversation between her, Jane Fonda and Candice Bergen, and I told her how impressed I was with the things she had to say about her mother—about how talented her mother was and how she had completely turned her back on her own career so that she could be supportive of her father's professional interests. I didn't realize it then, but my interest in her mother and what she had to say about her as a woman earned me her admiration and attention. Without realizing it, I was on the receiving end of another look—closer and longer.

We talked about our common Catholic backgrounds. While I was being kept after school at Our Lady of Angels for talking, her father was being summoned to Marymount Catholic Girls' School in Beverly Hills for the same reason.

While I was learning the Latin responses for serving Solemn High Midnight Mass on Christmas Eve, she was being ordered out of bed (during spiritual retreats at school) by a nun who grandly turned on the light in her room with the authoritative greeting *"Dominus vobiscum,"* and little Margaret Julia scrambled out of bed, quickly rubbed her eyes and blinked against the sudden assault of light, and as her hands fell stiffly to her sides and her nightie fell loosely to her ankles, this ten-year-old child of God blurted in a Pavlovian way, *"Et cum spiritu tuo."*

I also learned that ball-point pens were forbidden in California Catholic schools in the fifties, just as they were in Ohio.

The time for the show was approaching, and we were doing something for which both of us had been disciplined in school—we were talking, aloud and with enthusiasm, and at once. Her folks also used the word "gumption" when describing people of achievement. "Gallivanting" was another oft-used word in her house and in mine. (It was what your parents said you were doing when you didn't come home on time.)

As we made our way down the hall at WGN for the start of my program, I walked behind her and wondered how this glamorous TV/movie star with the bad-thought body could be so girl-next-door.

The show went very well. For both of us.

When she left, I wondered if I would ever see her again. I made no indication that I wanted to, and although she was very gracious I saw no signs that she was wondering about the same thing.

All the same, that afternoon I called her Chicago hotel, prepared to offer a well-rehearsed "Hey, you were great on my show today," only to be told that she wasn't in and asked, "Who's calling?"

I heard nothing from her that day, and when I retired that evening I knew she had my message, wasn't interested and, worse, was probably out "gallivanting" around Chicago.

The next day I met Bob Cromie in the hallway at WGN. He hosted *Book Beat* on the Public Broadcasting System and emceed his own discussion show on Saturday nights in Chicago. When I asked him who his guest was for that day's taping, he told me. "She's great," I said . . . and added, "I've got a crush on her."

Later that afternoon, Cromie stopped by my office to say, "She said *she's* got a crush on *you*." I thanked him for the report, gave the information some thought, reminded myself that my phoner had never been answered and concluded firmly that for all of her charm, she was capable of blarney and on this occasion her kind words about me had been just that.

Besides, Bob Cromie looked nothing like Cupid.

When I arrived home that night, a note next to the kitchen telephone, written in red ink and in Kevin's hand, read, *Marlo Thomas called.*

11

Journalism

The Chicago Television Emmy Awards, May 1979: "For the best spot coverage of a breaking story—The John Gacy Murders . . . The nominees are . . ."

John Wayne Gacy, a resident of suburban Chicago, was accused of murdering twenty-eight teen-age boys and young men after sexually assaulting them. The remains of most victims were found in his home —in the attic and in the crawl space under his living-room floor.

And there we were, anybody who is anybody in Chicago television, dressed to the teeth . . . and applauding and cheering wildly as the "winner" for Best Spot Coverage joyfully leaps to the stage to grab a local Emmy and breathlessly say "I wanna thank . . ."

To a journalist, good news is often not news at all. In the news business, tragedy is good business. The bloodier, the better. The more horrible the story, the greater the chance to demonstrate ability. A reporter's heart beats faster en route to a murder than it does en route to a City Hall meeting, and a journalist on television is more likely to receive an Emmy for covering mass murder than for covering local politics.

When I called the sheriff's office each morning back in Adrian, Michigan, or Dayton, Ohio, I was looking for deaths, not property-damage accidents. "I want fatals, gimme fatals." Journalists don't care about house fires, they care about *fatal* house fires. If it's a house fire in which children die, it is (Lord have mercy on me!) a *better* story.

"Banned in..."

Throughout the history of the *Donahue* program in syndication, there have been several examples of censorship exercised by the management at various *Donahue* television stations around the country. Following are some examples:

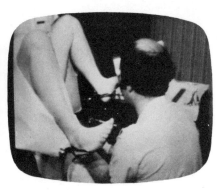

The Abortion Show, which included a film of an actual abortion: banned by WGN and approximately 10 percent of the total *Donahue* station lineup. "Too graphic."

Ray Kroc, founder of the McDonald's hamburger chain: banned by WNBC-TV in New York because we had placed the golden arches behind the millionaire and it "looked like a commercial."

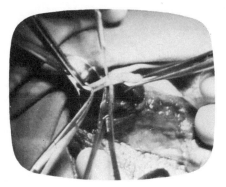

Reverse vasectomy and tubal ligation reconstruction: banned by WGN because it was "too educational for women . . . and too bloody."

Marian Burros, cookbook author: Banned by WNBC-TV because the kitchen demonstration showed a box of Minute Rice and it "looked like a commercial."

The Birth of a Baby: banned by approximately 5 percent of our stations, including WEWS-TV in my hometown of Cleveland. "Too graphic."

Screw magazine editor Al Goldstein: banned by WGN because of the word "screw" airing in the summertime when children might see it.

Lesbian mothers who won custody of their children: banned by KIRO in Seattle, Washington, because the fathers of the children had appealed the cases to higher courts.

Masters and Johnson: banned by KTVL in Medford, Oregon, because it "tantalized the audience by talking about homosexuality. This area is so conservative that programs like that get a lot of negative phone calls."

Mistresses Anonymous, featuring a mistress discussing the pain of dating married men: banned by WWLP in Springfield, Massachusetts.

Parents of Gays: banned by WWLP in Springfield, Massachusetts, because it was "a touchy issue to be dealt with during the summer months."

An expandable "penile implant" for male patients who suffer waist-down paralysis: banned from the *Today* show because "we don't like to discuss sex at that hour of the morning."

Photographs: Bob Hastings

The worse-is-better mentality takes hold early in a career and grows as the journalist grows. It escalates all the way to the "News Capital of the World," Washington, D.C., where the bronzed newspaper plates hanging in the austere lobby of the National Press Club are the front pages that screamed, JAPS BOMB PEARL HARBOR. And that is just the beginning of the lobby. Tragedy sells newspapers and earns—for some reporters—Pulitzer Prizes.

Adrenaline flows more profoundly through the body of a Washington reporter when she bangs out a lead like "Of John F. Kennedy's funeral it may be said, he would have liked it." (Mary McGrory)

Richard Nixon might be at least understood for wondering whether the adrenaline might have been flowing against him in the bodies of the men and women of the Washington press corps who, after all the speeches about objectivity and fairness, must acknowledge that they were "rewarded" professionally when he did not survive politically. If Nixon is impeached, or resigns, it becomes a world-stopping historic event. It becomes a banner headline, a six-column lead, a bronzed plate in the Press Club lobby. It becomes a *better* story.

My "better" stories in my first days as a journalist in Adrian were noticeably devoid of history-making headlines, so I did what I could with the tragedy and the pain at the local level. I once interviewed a father whose son, just minutes before, had drowned. I am belatedly repelled by how I was apparently more interested in the story than I was in the man's pain. Later, in Dayton, I interviewed the pilot of an F-104 that had flamed out after takeoff from Wright Patterson and slammed into a house (after he ejected), killing a little girl at play inside. At the scene I watched them pull her body out of the remains. I saw the chalk-white look of the dead that is so hard to describe. That night I interviewed the pilot and said, "You have children yourself, don't you?" And he wept when he replied, "Yes." At the time, I was proud of the interview; now I wonder why the Air Force made him available. After the interview was shown on the Dayton evening news, I received an angry postcard from a viewer who said, "Mike Wallace used to do that and that is exactly why he is no longer on the air." The hard-hitting *Mike Wallace at Large* had been cancelled a few weeks earlier. Mike Wallace was, and still is, one of my heroes. I recall being flattered by the comparison, but troubled and somewhat confused by the criticism.

I realize now that reporters seek out this kind of material for the same reason that people gather at auto accidents. (In Chicago a "gapers' block" is a traffic jam caused by motorists who slow down to "gape" at an accident in the opposite lane of traffic. Nothing physically obstructs the flow of traffic, only curiosity.) Reporters are the only people who benefit from this feature of the human condition. We are the "professional gapers," and if our work occasionally angers people it may be because all of us are somewhat uncomfortable with this feature of humanity.

In Dayton we once covered a tornado, interviewed people still in shock, some of them with house insulation still in their hair. In the background the viewer saw the place where the house had once stood, a pile of splinters. We would rush the dramatic footage ("It sounded like a train. I thought we were all dead") to the lab, edit it and bang out the script for a bulletin and then the longer, more detailed story for the evening newscast. Then we'd all go out for a beer and glory in the fact that we had beaten the competition by eight minutes, order more beer and go over the "great footage" we had. "Did you see the bike hanging in the tree?" The fact that scores of people that night were homeless or had lost all the property (if not loved ones) they had never occurred to us.

News personnel from a Chicago television station recently gathered in the bar of a private club following their daylong report on the crash of American Airlines Flight 191, which took the lives of 273 people. The tab for the booze was picked up by a grateful TV management person following what he thought was their outstanding coverage of the tragedy.

The point here is not that journalists want to see people die, or that reporters wish pain on other people. The point is to take note of the schizophrenic personality that develops within a community of competitive professionals whose enthusiasm heightens as the story becomes more horrible and who are rewarded for being first and for providing the most detail. (Chicago television reporters and TV critics spent much time and energy analyzing which channel had beaten which channel by how many minutes in reporting the death of Mayor Daley.)

The system often breeds an attitude that focuses on competition rather than comprehension. It also breeds insensitivity.

Several months after 165 people died in the Beverly Hills Night Club fire in northern Kentucky, singer John Davidson, the headliner on that tragic evening, told my television audience that he was appalled at the reporters who stuck microphones in the faces of people who were choking and inquired, "How do you feel?"

There is, across America, a dangerous but nevertheless growing animosity toward journalists. Part (not all) of the reasons for reporters' bad showing in public-opinion polls may be their bad showing in public manners.

Ask Spiro Agnew. On a recent *Donahue* show the former Vice-President grimly told the story of his brother's funeral, which took place on the day following his resignation: "It was a typical scrambling of photographers with hand-held cameras following me to the grave site," Agnew said. "Trampling over grave sites, knocking down floral arrangements, in one case tumbling a tombstone. And directional microphones sticking out to hear the conversation between my aunt and me at the car as I was trying to console her. That sort of thing. I think it was unnecessary."

What troubled me about his comments is my belief that if I had been there, I would have been one of the pack. There is no such animal as a managing editor who would welcome a reporter who returned to the office with no film, no pictures and no interviews, explaining, "Boss, I had too much respect for the grieving family." The reporter without the film and the pictures and the interview would also be without a job.

If a person is going to succeed in the marketplace, a sizable ego helps. It helps whether you are working at ITT, IBM or GE. But nowhere is ego more important or more manifest than at the bunch of letters known as CBS, NBC and ABC. If I were in Washington as a working reporter and saw a group of highly motivated, insecure and talented people all going after the same story, I'd try to get there first. Would I let a few tombstones get in the way of obtaining an interview and keeping the managing editor happy?

The crowd of reporters at the Agnew funeral recalls another unbecoming feature of modern American journalism. Much of the energy that makes Sammy the reporter run is not the inherent value of the story but how many other journalists are covering it. The "lemming feature" of the news business (See-the-President-get-into-the-helicopter; See-the-President-get-out-of-the-helicopter) distracts many reporters from other events like important (albeit boring) regulatory hearings on Capitol Hill which never become "news" because no reporter made them "news."

Penny Rotheiser from our office is in charge of dealing with the press. National magazines would not call her back until *Donahue* succeeded in New York. Now if *Newsweek* is preparing an article on our program, *Time* calls for an interview. During preparation for an article in *People, Us* magazine wants to know if Penny can "arrange a phoner with Phil."

Also calling are *TV Guide, Playboy, Esquire, Family Weekly,* the *National Catholic Reporter* and a host of other newspapers and magazines. Just hours after the *National Enquirer* phones to announce it's "doing a story on Phil," the *Star* calls with the same intention. (Penny is convinced that each newspaper has a spy in the other's editorial office.) News is not only what New York says is news; news is what other news people say is news. Journalism is "me-tooism." News copy is so often copied that Americans can rightly wonder what isn't being reported because all the journalists are out there chasing one another.

The insensitivity and "rat pack" look of journalists in public is by no means the only reason for their public disfavor. There is a more important reason. And it has nothing to do with reporters. It has to do with the insecurity of the public to whom they report. I believe much of the bad feeling Americans have for news personnel has to do with the nature of the product reporters are delivering. In short, Americans don't like the news, and like the angry impatient king, they are beheading the messenger. And happy-talk television newscasts are my industry's attempt to remedy this.

ANCHORMAN: "Here's Jack with the weather. Will I be able to play golf tomorrow?"

WEATHERMAN: "You're not able to play golf regardless of the weather."

Yuks from all the friendly, happy folks on the news set and more yuks from off camera. Sad. Even sadder, it works. Successful ratings for local newscasts are often determined not by the number of stories in the nightly newscast, but by the number of nightly yuks.

There is a place for awards in journalism; they encourage excellence and motivate other reporters. However, honors should be given to those who go it alone, rather than to those who are running with the pack. Recognition should come to the reporter who uncovers public cheating, or proves a convicted man innocent.

Presenting statues of honor to reporters for covering an earthquake is like presenting a first prize to a doctor for performing surgery. It is unbecoming, unprofessional and embarrassingly theatrical.

At a time when the press finds itself in public disfavor (and the "victim" of antipress decisions in the United States Supreme Court), reporters might well ask themselves whether the laughs in their newscasts are becoming more important than their stories and whether the clock has become more important than clarity. (Chicago residents are not well served by one television station "beating" another station by eight minutes in reporting the death of the Mayor.) The only people who care are the reporters themselves.

The Chicago Television Emmy Awards, May 1980: "For the best spot coverage of a breaking story—The Crash of American Airlines Flight 191 . . . The nominees are . . ."

12

Changes

SHE IS in the next-to-last row of my studio audience, seated with her hands folded in her lap, a little overweight. She is in her early 60s, and her hair has been carefully set and sprayed. Her coat rests either on her shoulders or on the back of her chair, and she stares straight ahead. At some moment during my warm-up, when I am moving about the audience, touching, joking, teasing, I will approach her and grasp her warm dry hands and say, "Are you going to help me? I'd help you if you had a show."

The people around her laugh, and she smiles and turns her head and eyes away from me, and I see her body retreat tightly within itself at just the thought that I might ask her to stand and take part in our program. I have seen this woman thousands of times in my studio audience, and I know there is no chance in the world that she will participate. She is a spectator and she always will be. She is millions of American women who grew up with their legs crossed and their minds closed by a culture that featured loud, intimidating men and silent, obedient women, who wash and can and sew and pray.

She functions in a society that bewilders her with its change. Since she went to church as a child, hat placed securely on the back of her head, white gloves in place, she has stoically lived through the fighting forties, the developing fifties, the angry sixties and the exhausting seventies. She knows there are dirty movies, pot, teen-age pregnancies and people living together without marriage, and she wonders when it will all end. She likes the pendulum metaphor, which says reassuringly, "It will swing back to the center again." But she's not so sure.

When she leaves, I say good-by to her, and if she says anything at all, she says, "How do you stand it here every day, with all these women?" Her feeling about women and her own self-loathing are apparent to me, but not to her. Her spirit has been smashed. It was smashed a long time ago, before she could know what happened.

It was smashed by a father who was always working outside the home and almost never sharing feelings inside it, her spirit smothered by an impatient mother who perhaps only once sat down with her and with dramatic exasperation undid the entire pot holder she had knitted so as to angrily teach her "the right way." It was smashed by a school system that expected her to be more silent, more obedient and more patient than the boys. It was smashed by folklore that encouraged her to long for boys without being able to do anything about it. She had to wait for an approach, never initiate one. At prom time, she waited for the phone to ring, and if it didn't she wasn't surprised. After all, who would want *her* for a date?

Finally, when one day a boy really did give her attention, she was so flattered, so excited, so overwhelmed, she grabbed him with both hands and, after being assured that her mother liked him, married him and has been sleepwalking through life with him ever since.

When she dies, she will leave a society that had more than sixty years (sometimes a lot more) to take advantage of her talent and failed to do so. Even sadder, she will have gone to the grave failing to realize most of her potential as a human being. Worse, she herself will never have even known the person she could have been. There may be mercy in her ignorance, but if what she doesn't know won't hurt her, it is killing us.

It is killing our society because we are failing to realize the potential contributions of at least half of the people who live in it. Feminists should not be alone in wondering what symphony wasn't composed, what medical breakthrough wasn't realized and what war wasn't stopped because the woman in the next-to-last row of my studio audience was "instructed" by countless examples offered by countless woman role models that the way to be in life is passive. Not a participant, but a spectator—with her hands folded in her lap.

Now comes her daughter. "I'm not a women's libber, but . . ." She loves her children, her girlfriends and her husband (sometimes in that order), and she is beginning, at age 35, to fight against a lifetime of programming, and to do some very nice things for, of all people, herself! She doesn't want a divorce . . . but . . .

She is most concerned about the quality of their relationship. She is increasingly aware of her husband's divided attention. When he talks to her it is more often on the telephone, and when he touches her it is more often in bed. She has very little information about his work, and that makes it more difficult for her to determine what it is that "seems to be bothering him." She is all the more frustrated by what appears to be his willingness to actually live this way without doing anything about it. Maybe it's hypoglycemia.

Maybe it's something a lot more complicated. Perhaps they got married because they wanted to have sex. Perhaps they got married because each perceived the other as good—in the *parents'* definition of the word. Perhaps they were pregnant. Perhaps they got married because that was what you did when you were that age. You got married. Everybody got married. Did we all get married at a time in life when we were least capable of making a lifetime decision?

Today's mother of 35 is doing a lot better job of relating to her children than her mother did. She has an easier time discussing menstruation with her daughter, but she is still not comfortable engaging the girl in conversation concerning sex and the pill and boys who want to "go all the way." When today's 40-year-old woman wasn't married at 22, her mother may have started a novena, but now that same woman wants her children to "wait a little while." When pressed for a definition of "little while," she may say, "Twenty-eight." When asked if she expects young people to remain celibate until that age, she smiles nervously and frankly confesses that she "doesn't know."

Today's mother is caught in the most dramatic shift in mores that has befallen any women in history.

She is running to stay abreast of change. She is curious about the women's movement but somewhat suspicious of its leaders. She thinks feminists "put down" housewives. She believes in equal pay for equal work, but she likes "to have doors opened for me." She thinks "femininity" is very important, but she is not sure what the word means. Underneath the speeches of the celebrity feminists she senses that after all the talk about "freedom of choice," "narrowly defined sexual stereotyping," "positive reinforcement" and "women as sex objects"— underneath all the speeches she senses that the celebrity feminist is looking her right in the eye and saying, "Baby, you've been had." And she resents it.

On days when her husband plays golf she resents the feminist speeches even more. Her resentment is often suppressed, and after all the socks are folded she may watch half of my program featuring a famous feminist and observe to herself that "she has no children." Then she sits down and writes a letter to me complaining about these "women's libbers," concluding with the words "I'm happy. I'm happy. I'm happy." Underlined in crayon.

She is also doing something else. She is working outside the home. Not because she wants luxuries, but because she wants food. Inflation is making it impossible to get through the days to her husband's next paycheck without being overdrawn at the bank. She feels guilty and she hates her job and she is being exposed to a lot of the sexist behavior that "libbers" talk about, but she is still "not a women's libber . . . but." The list of buts has grown longer, but she has not surrendered her ideal of God, motherhood and hot, steaming homemade apple pies. She wishes it could be that way again, but there just isn't time—and she is exhausted. But . . . she is happy. She is happy. She is happy. And you'd better believe it.

Now comes *her* daughter, the seventies teen-ager. Longer hair, no spray. Few skirts, lots of blue jeans. She does not can, nor does she sew. She not only looks at, but actually discusses out loud with other girls, flat and round boys' butts. If her mother danced dreamily to lyrics like

> A penny a kiss, a penny a hug
> I'm gonna save my pennies in a
> Little Brown Jug . . .

then today's teen-age daughter must certainly be dancing to:

> Oh Babe, I wanna kiss you all over.

She is taller than her mother, and her breasts are larger. She chews gum, smokes, drinks diet cola and is fat. She does not mind if boys call her "chick." She does not like school.

Today's teen-ager is not marriage-crazy. She wants to produce the local evening TV news. Her focus is definitely on boys, but not necessarily for immediate lifetime keeping. She is spending a lot more time talking and thinking about a career than her mother did. If Mr. Right comes along, that's fine—but he will be an addition to her career, not a replacement for it. They will discuss this thoroughly before they move in together, with or without marriage. Children? Later. Much later.

Today's teen-ager is "not a women's libber, but . . ."

She will be a member of the United States work force earlier and in greater numbers than her forebears. She will expect to succeed without really typing. She will also expect to be promoted with the same frequency and for the same reasons as men. When she succeeds in obtaining a job at the "entry level" of the large corporation, she will be in the company of millions of other young women just like her, and General Motors, IBM and Sears won't know what hit them.

The obedient "locked-in" stenographic pool will be gone forever, and so will the company budget that could count on long-term loyalty at predictable wages. Gone also will be the "12-hour-a-day man," and woman. These young people saw what workaholism did to their parents, and they will be hesitant to put all their life's eggs in the job basket. Men and women will expect time off for child-related responsibilities, like doctor and dentist appointments. And IBM will give them time off, grudgingly at first.

The result will be better mothers, better fathers, better marriages and happier children.

When the last joke is told by the last good ol' boy at the bar—and when the last whistle is heard by the passing woman at a construction site—the Movement will still be here. It has brought and will continue to bring some of the greatest changes any culture has ever known.

By the year 2000, the *Donahue* audience will no longer be predominantly female. Chairs will be occupied by both men and women, in equal numbers. Husbands and wives will share the responsibilities not only of "bringing home the bacon" but of "bringing up the baby" as well. We will, all of us, be the beneficiaries of the courage of the feminists of the early sixties who were out there, almost alone, being ridiculed by a male-dominated press, laughed at by people who were threatened by their message. Without their conviction, their love and their anger, women might still in the year 2000 be seated in the next-to-last row of my studio audience, silent, eyes straight ahead, hands folded in their laps, saying to themselves, over and over again, as in prayer:

"I'm happy. I'm happy. I'm happy."

13

The Staff

THE ONLY thing more challenging, more frustrating, more maddening than walking out there every day of the week and smiling for the audience is working for a person who does this daily "approve-of-me" exercise for a living. The people in the *Donahue* office in Chicago have dealt with me in a way that should be expected only of a mother. They have fought patiently for my attention during my moments of preoccupation before programs and after some bad ones. They have seen me mad, sad and glad and dealt evenly with all three.

The people in my office *are* the show. Their minds are the source of what finally gets on the air, and of how it will be presented. More than Carson needs DeCordova, more than Jimmy needs Rosalynn, I need them. I simply do not have 240 program ideas a year that will effectively compete with *Card Sharks, Ryan's Hope* and reruns of *All in the Family*. When, prior to my departure on a recent skiing vacation, Dick Mincer, the executive producer of our program, said, "Don't kill yourself; I don't want to have to break in another one," I laughed only a little bit.

As a living, it probably beats parking cars, but working for me isn't for everybody. Here are some of the people who have survived the experience and whose own lives will never be the same. In spite of the pressure (or perhaps because of it), these loyal staffers have grown and been enriched by the experience of making decisions that determine what millions of Americans see on *Donahue* every day of the year.

Dick Mincer, the executive producer of *Donahue,* saw the spotlight and heard the sound of applause earlier in life and more often than I did. As a child, Dick sang in the Columbus Boychoir School. From the ages of 10 through 14 he traveled around the country in a bus, specially equipped with desks for schooling, and sang in every state in the Union. In the early fifties he performed on the *Paul Whiteman Show,* the *Dan Seymour Show* and the *Don Ameche and Frances Langford Show,* and on one occasion he entertained Albert Einstein in the living room of the scientist's home.

He pursued his broadcasting career at Ohio State University, and after graduating in 1961 he worked at WBNS-TV in Columbus. In 1965 he moved to Dayton, Ohio, and WLW-D, and in October of 1967 he became the first producer/director of *The Phil Donahue Show.*

In the twelve years that *Donahue* has been on the air, Dick has summoned an ambulance for Sammy Davis, Jr., when he appeared to be having a heart attack (it was indigestion); personally escorted Muhammad Ali out of a crowded auditorium and into a private plane for an appearance on our program the next day; gently ordered Linda Lovelace to wear another blouse when she failed to pass his TV breast test; single-handedly talked the president of General Motors into debating his most powerful adversary, Ralph Nader; refused to touch the electric chair in the Ohio State Penitentiary during a camera setup for one of our shows and thrown his body in front of a high school band so it wouldn't overwhelm Anita Bryant, who was singing "How Great Thou Art" to my nearby audience at the Ohio State Fair. Dick Mincer chooses remote locations for our telecasts, answers budget questions from suspicious management personnel and deals remarkably well with the insecurities of the man whose name appears on the program he has been working with for the past twelve years.

Dick's own emotional maturity has been sharpened by his constant dealing with second-banana status, and it has been confirmed on those many occasions when, after the initial flurry of greetings and attention directed at me, people will sooner or later turn and say to Dick, "So you're Phil's executive producer. What does an executive producer do?"

Let him tell you.

MINCER:

I suppose that of all of the people in the office I'm asked the most frequently, "What do you do?" or "What does an executive producer do?" There was a time twelve years ago when I produced and directed the show, and the answers seemed much simpler then. As the only male producer in our office, I have lent Phil my belt, socks, a couple of ties, a shirt and even my pants so that the show could go on.

Having been with the program from the very beginning, I think there is a part of me involved in each show that we do. While the show is being directed, and has been for the last six years, by Ron Weiner, I know that some of the directing techniques I developed in Dayton are still being used today. The three producers in the office have, in at least some small way, adopted some of my methods (begging, cajoling and even angering) for booking a show and then being able to save it or keep it booked if it looks as if the guest might cancel.

Presenting five sixty-minute shows each week entails an enormous amount of work. Each guest must be hoteled, and airplane reservations must be made. An audience has to be booked. The stations that air our show around the country must receive advance information for promotion.

Letters from viewers, good and bad, must be read and answered. An engineering crew has to be prepared for each day's happening. The video recordings that we make of each show must be duplicated and sent to the stations that air us, and the videotapes have to find their way home after their last play. For each show to work completely, each of these functions must be carried out, and there must be contingency plans when something breaks down. I am the person in the center of those plans. Rarely does it all happen without a hitch. There is almost always some problem that must be solved, and the executive producer must be a part of the solution. In my case it certainly does not mean that I have all of the answers, or that my word is law. I think in the family situation that has developed over the history of our show that such an individual would find himself in an unworkable relationship. Rather, it is a collective approach to finding a solution and then putting that solution into action.

One of the most enjoyable things that has happened to the staff of the *Donahue* show is that stations in various parts of the country that carry our program invite us to their city to present a week of shows. For us it means getting away from the office, breaking the routine—and let's be honest: when everything goes well, it can be a mini vacation. We've been to San Diego, Atlanta, Pittsburgh, New York, Philadelphia and dozens of other cities. The audiences are overwhelming. The local station personnel treat us like the Second Coming, and we are wined and dined in a first-class manner all week. Obviously, we look forward to going on these trips.

One of my jobs is to visit the host station several weeks in advance and choose a site for the telecast, check hotel accommodations and go over the requirements for our show. As good as these remotes can be, there are exceptions. For a week in Miami (several years ago) we had booked the following guest lineup:

Monday—Cass Elliot
Tuesday—Sammy Davis, Jr.
Wednesday—Monty Hall
Thursday—Susan Saint James
Friday—Rona Barrett

Heavy on the performers, and different from most *Donahue* weeks, but it seemed to fit the Miami mood.

I planned to leave from Dayton on Friday morning, one day in advance of the rest of the staff, to ensure that everything was in a state of readiness. Thursday night, an unknown voice from the Promotion Department at ABC-TV called to inform me that Monty Hall, of *Let's Make a Deal* fame, was canceling his appearance because his schedule was too tight. I pleaded with the caller to let me phone Hall and talk to him, but network people are not in the habit of giving out phone numbers of stars. He did promise, however, that he would get in touch with Hall's producer and that *maybe* he would call me. Fifteen minutes later Hall's producer was on the phone and I was pleading my case. "He's the only guest for an hour." "We'll have a big studio audience and no guest." "All of our promotion for the week has been released." "He's my mother's favorite!" I said every line I could think of to get Hall to reconsider, and finally I begged (as one producer to another) to talk to Hall and explain our predicament. An hour later Monty Hall called me and said that he was sorry for whatever inconvenience he might have caused, didn't realize what a bind he was placing us in and yes, he would come to Miami for our show. I went to bed with a deep sense of personal satisfaction and no inkling of what lay in store.

The next morning at the Dayton airport I checked in at the counter to have my ticket validated and a large menu board with the flight schedules caught my eye. All the flights listed said ON

TIME except mine which said SEE AGENT. There had been a sky-jacking attempt at the Baltimore Airport, delaying several flights. I finally arrived in Miami at 7:30 P.M., only to discover that my luggage had gone to that great baggage claim in the sky. No suits, no underwear, no toothbrush, no nothin'. (I firmly believe that when my luggage is lost, it flies to more exciting places than I do.) I was met at the airport by the local station's promotion director, George White, who promptly informed me that a recent newscast had disclosed that our opening guest, Cass Elliot, had become seriously ill in California and had canceled all her appearances. This time it would do me no good to call Cass and beg my case. She was sick, and I was stuck.

Lainie Kazan was appearing at the Deauville Hotel that week, so I raced over to see the show and then went backstage to see what I could do. I explained the situation (actually, she was appearing at the Deauville as Cass's replacement), and she agreed to appear on our program. Normally that would have allowed me a good night's sleep, but for some reason, lost luggage always appears at your hotel at 3 A.M., and for some other reason, hotel clerks always call you at 3 A.M. to ask if you want your luggage.

And now a word about the hotel. The Barcelona Hotel had two elevators which, when both were operating at the same time (which they never were) held a maximum of twelve people—six on each—no more. If seven people got on the one working elevator, a buzzing noise would begin, and the door would not close, and the elevator would remain in place. Guests were actually arguing about who had got on last and who had to get off. As the week progressed, the *Donahue* staff would find that the easiest way up or down was the stairs. On the third day the entire hotel phone system went out and stayed out for the rest of the week. Much of the time no one could call in or out. For a show like ours which depends on the phone and for our staff, who think that Alexander Graham Bell had us in mind when he invented it, being without telephones is a disaster. We spent a lot of time in pay phones that week—which wasn't all bad, since the phone booths were cleaner than our rooms. Susan Saint James, our guest for Thursday, was the only one who was staying at that hotel with us. Susan changed rooms once because the first one was so dirty; then, seeing that changing rooms made no difference, she stayed where she was. But she didn't forget the experience, and it took us three years to persuade her to do the show again. Somehow we survived the Barcelona.

Tuesday's guest was Sammy Davis, Jr. Sammy arrived about an hour and a half early, which is highly unusual, since most of our guests do not show up until about fifteen minutes before air time. However, I discovered that Sammy was early because he was experiencing chest pains and wanted to lie down. We took him upstairs to a conference room and placed him on a couch. The pains got worse, and Sammy requested an ambulance. Within minutes a Miami emergency squad was on the scene, and after a brief examination they decided that Sammy might be having a heart attack. Thirty minutes before air time our guest was placed on a stretcher and wheeled away to a hospital. I couldn't believe what was happening to us. Shortly before Sammy's arrival I had been introduced to Mel Tormé, who had been visiting the studio. We all went rushing off looking for Mel and fortunately found him waiting outside, about to get into his limo. I explained what had happened to Sammy and asked him if he would pinch-hit, and he did.

At the end of the week I accompanied Phil and the other members of the staff to a radio show on which Donahue was to be interviewed. While Phil sat next to the show's host, all of us on the staff were watching in the audience. During a commercial break, Phil introduced us. When the commercial ended and the program resumed, the host came to me, stuck his microphone in my face and said, "What does an executive producer do?"

And I couldn't think of an answer.

We go to great effort to book guests for the *Donahue* show, and if the guest is Muhammad Ali, the effort has to be "the greatest."

Ali had never been on *Donahue*. He was coming to Dayton for a Black Expo and accepted our invitation to do our program the same morning. He was speaking the night before in Hartford, Connecticut. I said to the contact at the Expo, "We'll meet him at the Dayton airport." The guy said, "He's not flying. He's driving, because he's afraid to fly."

I remember thinking, It's a fourteen-hour drive; he'll never make it. This was the day before the show, and I was panicked. I chartered a plane, took the sports director of our station along and flew to Hartford with the understanding that Ali would fly back with us. That night, Ali delivered his speech for the college students, then went back to his hotel to get something to eat. That was okay, except there were four or five men with Ali, hangers-on. They didn't want him to leave; they wanted to party all night.

Now I was really getting nervous. They kept stalling and stalling. It was past midnight and we had a four-hour flight. Suddenly I remembered that he was afraid to fly, so I lied. "Excuse me, Champ, but the pilot told me there's a storm coming in from the east and we'd better get out of here in fifteen minutes or we're going to have rough flying." With that he bolted to the door and we all left for the airport.

He was indeed a fearful flier. He strapped himself in and could not seem to clutch the armrests tightly enough. I was amazed: the heavyweight champion of the world—terrified. Fortunately, it was a smooth flight, and we were in the air only fifteen minutes before Muhammad was in the cockpit and the crew was allowing him to "fly" the plane. We arrived as the sun was coming up, but we made it.

Pat McMillen is the senior producer of the *Donahue* program. She never had any desire to have children, and didn't. She did marry her high school sweetheart. The marriage lasted eleven years, "most of which was a very happy time in my life," she says. During the early years of her marriage she worked as a secretary while her husband held down a good job as a skilled tradesman.

McMillen:

We had a house, two cars and a boat; what more could I want? So I quit my job and became a full-time housewife. After I had visited all my friends, shopped, sewed, read and done all the other things a working woman doesn't have time to do, I was climbing the walls, watching TV and hooked on soap operas. One day while sitting in the doctor's office for the fourth or fifth time with one of my girlfriends and her child, I realized that I was fast becoming a shuttle service for friends whose husbands had taken their only car to work. That's when I checked the want ads and promptly showed up for an interview with George Resing, program director of WLW-D in Dayton, Ohio. Some time later, Phil Donahue would join the station and I would be assigned to work for him. None of us had any idea at that time what was coming. What I did know was that my life as a stay-at-home housewife had come to an end. It had lasted three months.

For the first couple of years, Pat was the secretary. She typed booking orders, confirmed airline reservations for guests and wrote thank-you letters. Then after several feminists appeared on our show, Pat made her move. Why, she wanted to know, couldn't she help produce the show rather than just perform the narrower, less challenging clerical duties of the program?

When I stop to consider how central Pat's contribution to the success of our program is, I am embarrassed to recall that she actually had to ask my permission to give the show her uniquely creative energies. Today she is one of the most sought-after and powerful women in broadcasting. Her phone rings all day long.

Pat is an only child, raised in Arcanum, Ohio. Her father raced trotting horses as a hobby, and Pat remembers the day all the men snickered at a woman, a black woman, who showed up at the track to—of all things—race with the men. Pat said she got goose bumps when that woman won a race. Pat also admits to having "tears in my eyes" when many years later she saw Janet Guthrie wave from behind the wheel of her race car as she roared by three hundred thousand people at the Indianapolis 500.

McMillen's feminist pride does not manifest itself only in tears and goose bumps. She once led a strike of women at our television station in Dayton protesting low wages. (The effort earned her a "small" pay hike.) On another occasion, it was suggested that the daily coffeepot should be prepared by everyone in the office, not just the women. Pat explains what happened:

McMILLEN:

You wouldn't believe the ruckus. And all over a pot of coffee. The men said they didn't have time to make it. One argued that because he didn't drink it he should not have to make it. Another, who drank it, said he was going to quit coffee rather than assume the responsibility of brewing it. The "crisis" ended when the program moved to Chicago and the *Donahue* office contracted with the WGN cafeteria for one already-perked pot of coffee per day. Nevertheless, the secretaries in the office usually pick up the coffee and carry it to the office, and there's an occasional fuss over who goes most often. Clearly, making and/or retrieving coffee is seen as "women's work," and any attempt to change that risks the start of World War Three.

On one occasion a male staffer in our office developed the habit of having a recently hired secretary pour his coffee for him. He would place his cup next to the pot and return to his desk to await delivery of the refilled cup, with cream and sugar added and stirred. I told the secretary to stop that service immediately, and another woman in the office threatened to break her arm if she continued. Her response was "But I've been doing it. How can I tell him I'm not doing it anymore?" We said, "Just stop doing it." The first day or two, he brought out his cup, returned to his office and waited. After a few minutes he returned to the coffee area, walked around actually stalking the cup, looking first at the coffee, then at the secretary. (She later said she felt very uncomfortable.) Finally, he realized that as far as he and the coffee were concerned, he was on his own.

There are other signs of sexism in our office. When male office members go out of town on business, they arrange for limousines to take them to the airport, while the women in the office must provide their own transportation.

There's also a locker-room mentality about the men. They often get together behind closed doors for meetings, but if the women all get together in a room we are usually interrupted by one of the men and we are questioned about "what's going on in here." Unless it's personal, the women in the office are made to feel they shouldn't close the door.

On one occasion women staffers placed a male nude centerfold on the wall. When Phil and Dick saw it they almost fainted and insisted it be removed. We argued that male technicians often place girlie pictures on the walls of their work areas; why couldn't we have the same freedom with male photos? After another males-only powwow, the women were ordered to take the poster down. The men's long explanation did not include the biggest reason for their decision. The poster made them feel uncomfortable.

One of the most challenging shows Pat ever produced dealt with abortion.

McMILLEN:

Several years ago a friend of mine became pregnant by a married man. She called me, totally panicked. At the time, New York State was the nearest place to get a legal abortion. The only alternative at the time was the so-called "back-street butcher." I felt at a total loss. I had no idea whom to call about an abortion, and I had no idea what actually happened to you when you got one. I tried to calm her down and said I'd be right over. She said she was thinking about suicide and hung up.

I drove to her house and, after knocking on the door several times, broke in—and couldn't find her. I called the police and waited anxiously for four hours before she returned. After several phone calls, we found a safe clinic in New York State. I drove her to the airport and waited nervously for her return that night. I was frightened by my ignorance. What were they doing to her? When she got off the plane that night, I was so relieved to see her walking unassisted that I cried.

I thought about that experience when we decided to make the attempt to film an actual abortion. After much research I found a safe, responsible clinic in Chicago and set up a meeting with Phil, myself and the operators of the clinic. After assuring them that we would be responsible (not sensational) and would protect the anonymity of the patient, we obtained legal releases from the patient and were present with our camera when the abortion candidate showed up with her boyfriend.

The woman who had agreed to be filmed was in her first trimester. She was 26 and divorced, and while married she had borne two children, one of whom had been given up for adoption. Her boyfriend paid $150 in cash. The year was 1975. I remained in the treatment room with our cameraman; Phil waited in the lobby. Two nurses held the woman's hand while the doctor dilated the cervix, then turned on a small motor that created a vacuum in a small hoselike instrument that is inserted in the vaginal canal. The technique is called vacuum suction curettage.

Despite the noise of the motor, I remained calm as the so-called "birth matter" came through a clear plastic tube and into a glass bottle. The nurses kept up their small talk. (No doubt our camera provoked some "grandstanding." It is doubtful that every patient got as much personal attention as our TV subject.) Suddenly there was a loud swooshing sound. Our cameraman, perspiring profusely and carefully shooting from the side to avoid "vaginal exposure," had backed into a wall sink and his foot hit a floor pedal, which in turn caused the water to rush out of the spigot.

Suddenly, I felt I was about to faint. I thought, Oh no, not here! It could panic the patient (not to mention the doctor) if I keeled over, so I backed up and placed my hands against the cold ceramic tile on the wall and then loosened my collar. I didn't faint, but I could feel beads of perspiration on my forehead and queasiness in my stomach.

The entire process took only seven minutes. I will always remember the woman's first comment when it was over: "Gee, I thought I would automatically die or something when it happened, and I'm not dead at all." The comment supported my view that more women needed a lot more information about what went on in the actual abortion procedure.

Later, when Phil showed the film to Right to Life people in Chicago, one of the women in the room wept and in near-hysteria begged him not to use it on television. She was convinced that the apparent simplicity of the technique (and its brevity) amounted to a commercial for abortion. Phil argued that what we had filmed was the way it is, and that ignorance is not bliss and that to deny this information to people was "the kind of thing they do in Russia." Besides, he was inviting the Right to Life spokespersons to appear on the show to share their views with the television audience. They finally agreed, and a balanced program, featuring the filmed abortion and statements of opposition (complete with photos of discarded fetuses in wastebaskets), was sent to all the television stations that carried *Donahue*.

Approximately 10 percent of the *Donahue* stations refused to carry the program, including WGN. They used words like "too graphic" and "in bad taste" to support their decision. Joining the fight to get the program on the air in Chicago were the people of the Right to Life community, who, when they saw the final version of the show, looked upon it as tilted in favor of the "prolifers."

My own personal opinion changed after I saw the actual abortion. Before the show, I would without hesitation or counseling have had an abortion and not given it a second thought. After seeing it, I would have more seriously considered the alternatives. The decision might still be to abort, but at least I'd be making a better decision with much more information.

I still think it should be the decision of the woman involved whether or not she gets an abortion, but certainly an informed decision will be better than the panicky choice made by people like my friend who rushed to an abortion clinic in fear and in ignorance.

Pat also remembers several incidents that were exasperating, humorous and memorable.

McMILLEN:

On a remote in Atlanta, I was assigned to drive Maharishi Mahesh Yogi, the Beatles' guru, from his retreat house to the studio. His followers were very strict about the car he would ride in. It had to be cleaned and aired and have incense burned in it so there would be no lingering tobacco smoke. He would ride in the front seat, and only silk or natural hide could touch his body.

When I arrived, incense was burned and a silk cloth was placed over the seat back and a goatskin over the seat. He got into the front seat next to me and sat in a Lotus yoga position with his feet tucked under him. Three of his people climbed into the back seat. I prayed that this would be one of the safest drives of my life.

About a mile from the studio, the driver in front of me slammed on his brakes for no apparent reason. I slammed on my brakes and automatically threw out my right arm, as a mother does to protect a child on the front seat. I hit the Maharishi with a thud, pinning him against the back of his seat. His people in back almost jumped into the front seat to make sure I hadn't injured him. I apologized profusely. All the Maharishi did was sit there and giggle.

I never get over the phone calls and letters from our viewers. One man sent a letter enclosing a $100 check and asked us to forward it to the Ohio State Penitentiary, where we had done our show the preceding week. He told us he wanted to help the prisoners. When O.S.P. attempted to cash the check, it bounced. The warden told us this had happened before. I can't imagine why anyone would bother to perform a kindly deed knowing it was a farce.

A woman wrote us after a doctor had discussed celibacy on the show and asked us to rush her the doctor's name and address because her husband had caught this dread disease. She knew from the symptoms. Somehow I think she must have missed some of the discussion.

I had tears in my eyes after reading the following letter:

10/25/78

Dear Ms. McMillen:

Have received your letter on the 27th of September, the day after mine and my spouses Fourty-seventh wedding anniversary.

It was a quiet Tuesday, a little overcast and no anniversary congratulating.

That evening we had received a long distance call from our older daughter in Phoenix, quite distraught over an impending divorce. That added fear to our loneliness.

She and her physician husband have four lovely, healthy daughters, our pride and joy.

Receiving your letter was a ray of light that brightened my day, that someone has not forgotten.

                                        Sincerely yours,

The saddest thing is that the letter these lonely people received from me that made them feel so good was a form letter.

One day in Pittsburgh, when we were taping the show outdoors, a woman holding a baby stood up to ask a question. The baby's face was covered with a red workman's handkerchief—to keep the sun out of its eyes, Phil thought. He decided to show the baby's face on TV. What a shock when he lifted the kerchief and exposed not only the baby's sweet face, but the mother's breast while the baby nursed. For once in his life, Phil was speechless.

One December 31, Phil decided to show how the increased intake of alcohol slows a person's reaction time—just in case anyone was planning to drink and drive on New Year's Eve. He got a breathometer machine, a policeman to administer the test on the air and a willing subject. You guessed it: The more the man drank, the faster his reactions became.

Sometimes older people write very dear letters and you can easily tell how trapped, lonely and helpless much of today's older population must feel. One lady wrote to Phil enclosing a $3 personal check. The only thing she asked for was that Phil send her the name of a good laxative. She said she was older and had been taken advantage of many times, even by her doctor, and she was afraid to go out much. Now, she watched Phil every day and trusted him. The letter wasn't a hoax. Phil sent the check back to her with a note saying it wouldn't be wise of him to prescribe a laxative and suggested that she get someone to recommend a good doctor. She sent a thank-you note apologizing for placing Phil in such an awkward position.

Women used to wear girdles, and one day I had on one that pinched so badly I hurried into the powder room to remove it before our guest, the late William Lear, the man who perfected the Lear jet, arrived. Darlene Hayes stood by the door to take the girdle and throw it into my desk drawer so I wouldn't have to walk out with it in my hand when I greeted Mr. Lear. Well, the guest arrived a couple of minutes early and got past the receptionist without being announced. Hearing his footsteps in the hall, Darlene went to investigate. The guest walked in ahead of Darlene. I heard the footsteps too, and thinking it was Darlene handed my girdle out the door to William Lear.

At a dinner of high-powered business moguls in Miami, Pat and Producer Darlene Hayes showed up each wearing a pink dress. During my speech I introduced them as "my two pink princesses." I will never forget the look on their faces, and they will never let me forget the incident. Not only did I call them princesses (meaning pampered, passive and pretty), I actually conveyed a sense of ownership by using the word "my." Worse, Darlene is not pink, she is black, and never ever wanted to be any other color.

Darlene grew up in Topeka, Kansas, surrounded by her six brothers. As the only girl in the family, Darlene received a lot of attention, a lot of love and a lot of unsolicited advice. When she was 8, her brother "taught" her how to drive a motorcycle, and she promptly drove it into the side of a neighbor's house.

Darlene's first personal exposure to racism came when her junior high friend Betty (a white girl) suddenly stopped talking to her when

35. Atheist Madalyn Murray O'Hair in one of her earliest appearances on the show. She was the first guest on *The Phil Donahue Show* when it began in Dayton on November 6, 1967.

36. Ralph Nader—December 12, 1972.

37. Jerry Rubin—April 1, 1970.

38. Gloria Steinem—January 9, 1970.

39. Bella Abzug—August 11, 1972.

40. Anita Bryant—March 9, 1977.

41. Liv Ullmann—April 8, 1976.

42. Senator Hubert Humphrey—June 7, 1976.

43. Bob Hope—June 16, 1976.

44. Then heavyweight champion Joe Frazier at Ohio State Penitentiary—
November 8, 1971.

45. Neither I nor the elephant "will ever forget" Niagara Falls—May 14, 1974.

46. Belly dancing with Zia—May 7, 1974.

47. Cooking lesson—February 10, 1976.

48. Roller skating with the "Thunderbirds," an all-female Roller Games team—May 21, 1975.

49. Mel Brooks—Chicago's Navy Pier, August 2, 1976.

50. Walter Matthau and George Burns—December 19, 1975.

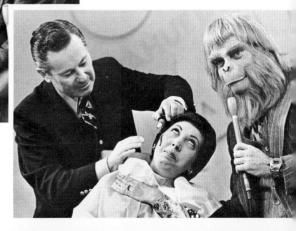

51. Make-up expert Frank Westmore "scarring" an audience member while the host "goes ape"—April 29, 1976.

52. Gerald Ford—May 18, 1979.

53. Ronald Reagan—March 15, 1977.

they entered high school. She feels hurt to this day and still re-members high school as a place where white students gathered to so-cialize on one floor while the black students congregated on another. Today, Darlene is enjoying her second marriage and is raising two children by her first marriage, Robert, 13, and Toi, 11.

During the ten years that Darlene has been with our show, we have spent several days in most of America's major cities during what we call "remote weeks." For Darlene, the longest week of her professional life was spent in Miami Beach, a place where blacks work and whites vacation. On one occasion she was returning from a shopping trip and a white man followed her down Collins Avenue, into the hotel lobby and onto the elevator. Only when she faced him and voiced a firm profanity did he realize that she wasn't a hooker. She was ill at ease when she passed black maids in the hotel hallway. "I'm very uncom-fortable when I approach a black person who is working on her knees," Darlene has told me. "Do I speak? I don't want her to think that I believe I'm better than she is." Noticing that she was the only black person staying at the hotel, an old lady walked up to Darlene and said, "Who are you, a singer or something?" During our remote weeks in Miami Beach, she almost never leaves her room.

Darlene has had some really scary experiences in the course of working on our show. Let her tell you about the street gang.

HAYES:

> When Pat was producing a program dealing with gang violence, I wanted to go out and film so I could get more insight into what they were about. It was arranged for me to meet a street worker named Ken who was to get permission to bring our camera onto the "turf" of a gang. I don't know what I expected to see—cer-tainly not all those clean-faced young men who acknowledged themselves as gang members. All the gangs we met we found on school playgrounds. As we greeted each gang, Ken introduced me as a producer for *Donahue*. Every one of those kids knew the *Donahue* show.
>
> It soon became apparent that these kids were serious about their gang activity and capable of hurting someone. They greeted us with "Shorty got shot four times; he's in intensive care." "Romeo got picked up by the cops for beating some guy in the head with a golf club." Two boys about 13 and 14 told Ken that

their 19-year-old brother was in prison for murdering a rival gang member. At one playground, two kids ran to a trash can, then to Ken's van. Ken said, "I saw you stash your piece [gun]." They never denied it. Instead they said, "Well, you know . . ."

They were like men/children. Very excited about being on television, one kept shouting, "Phil Donahue's gonna make me a star." When I asked if I could interview him on camera, he said I couldn't show his face because he'd then become a target for a rival gang. I asked him if he was afraid he might get killed. He said he wasn't afraid to die because when you start getting scared, that's when someone gets you. I found out later that several of his friends, no older than 22, were already dead.

When we arrived for the filming, some policemen were arresting the three young men who'd said they'd go on our show. The charges were intimidation and disorderly conduct. The club members had brought their sweaters to show us. Each gang has its own color and symbols. If a member is wearing his sweater, that means he's looking for a fight. If it's folded and carried over his arm, he's coming in peace. The three young men who were arrested had their sweaters over their arms. They told the officers they'd brought the sweaters because they were being interviewed by us. I felt very guilty. I also had ambivalent feelings about where good journalism ends and exploitation begins. All three went to jail. Two were let out that same evening without a fine, but the other spent the night in jail and had to pay $30 to get out.

Media people sometimes get caught up in sensationalism and we forget that people are being affected by what we do. We sometimes even play right into the hands of attention seekers. One kid pointed to a graffitied wall, saying, "Take my picture with this; I did this one." Another yelled, "This is Stone City. We the baddest mothers around." Another showed us the knifing scars on his stomach as if they were badges of honor. Right beside the biggest scar, from mid chest to below his navel, was a healed bullet wound.

Nothing I'd read in the newspaper or seen on TV had given me the real sense of commitment, fear and isolation of gang members that I got by being there. I tried to carry those feelings back to Phil to keep our exploration of gang involvement from becoming sensational and insensitive to the way people live from day to day.

Men find Darlene very attractive. But she seldom says yes to dinner invitations offered by males who guest on our show. Seldom. Not never.

HAYES:

I found Richard Pryor to be a very complicated and interesting man. When I first saw him in the warm-up room, he looked much smaller than I had imagined. This man, who could bare his ass on stage, actually looked reserved and shy. After the introduction and light conversation, he let his road manager do most of the talking. When Phil came in, Pryor told him how much he enjoyed the show and was looking forward to doing it. Phil briefed him and very gently reminded him that we were a daytime TV show and to be careful with his language.

Mr. Pryor was very polite, and when we left the room for the studio, he saw that everyone else went out the door first. En route down the hall he told me he saw our "criticism show," during which the producers had publicly defended the decision to put black activist Florence Kennedy on the show. (Viewers were enraged when she sang her own parody of "My Country, 'Tis of Thee [Sweet land of bigotry]." There are angry viewers who have not watched our program since that day.) Pryor said he liked the way the producers defended the questions that came to us about that show.

The program with Pryor was being taped for later broadcast. The studio audience was unusually small for the 9:30 A.M. taping. (The program is usually live at 11 A.M. in Chicago.) The show started off very slowly with Phil clumsily doing some of Richard's material, and Richard was not helping him at all. Phil kept fishing and trying to find something that would turn Richard on. Finally Phil said, "What do you and your friends sit around on Saturday nights and talk about—like, you know, when the guys get together?" Richard answered, "Pussy," and Phil's face turned tomato red. The few black people in the audience laughed nervously; the white women, mostly suburban middle-class housewives, did not move a muscle.

Phil, perspiring, moved on to other subjects. Richard opened up a little when he talked about growing up in Peoria and about the people who were the center of many of his comedy routines.

Everything appeared to be going a little smoother until Phil approached an attractive 50-ish white woman for her question.

"I used to really enjoy *Amos 'n' Andy*," she said, "and I was just wondering why black people don't accept them and don't want any of their reruns shown on TV today."

Richard, mimicking an old person, said, "You're old and you're going to die soon, so why should you care?"

Phil tried to cover the insult by saying, "Come on, Richard, you know what she means; you make your living by telling stories about people like Amos and Andy."

At the close of the show, Phil said, "Well, thanks, Richard. It's really been an interesting hour." Whereupon Richard said, "Fuck you, Phil."

Everyone in the studio was uncomfortable. No one knew whether he was joking or not. I had no reading on how Phil felt, nor was I sure how Richard felt. (The Pryor show aired with the profanity bleeped.) Whenever Phil makes a personal appearance, the question of how he felt during the Richard Pryor show always comes up. His answer: "Uncomfortable."

I waited after the taping to escort Pryor to his limousine. As soon as the show ended, Pryor returned to his off-stage personality—shy, polite and soft spoken. He thanked the audience for being there and expressed gratitude to the black women who said they liked his albums.

He did not say a word to me until we reached the car. As he was about to get into the back seat he turned to me and said, "I'd like to take you to dinner." I was shocked, but recovered enough to say, "Sure."

That night, he bought a rose for me en route to dinner, and held the limousine door when we entered and exited the vehicle. Boy, he was charming.

At dinner he did not talk about himself. He wanted to know where I was from, how I got with Phil, my family, children. I couldn't believe this was the man who had said "Fuck you" to my boss in front of an entire studio audience only hours before.

At dinner he ordered caviar, which was served on a small dish perched on top of the head of a swan sculptured from a block of ice. It was turning into a very pleasant evening. After some early anxiety about how I looked and what I was wearing, I was beginning to relax and really enjoy myself.

Across the aisle from our table, a sexy woman with long,

flowing blond hair, wearing a low-cut one-piece black pants outfit, kept looking at Richard. Finally, she got up, came over to our table and with no "excuse me" said to Richard, "Hi. I know you're a big fan of mine, so I thought I would bring you *my* autograph." She handed him a piece of paper with something written on it. She meant no harm. But she was impolite, and it was a bad joke.

"Do you see this young lady and I are sitting here trying to have a conversation?" Richard said. "Why would you come over here and disturb us? Now get the fuck away from the table."

"I was only kidding," she said. "You don't have to get so damn nasty."

"Kidding or not, you are disturbing me. Now get the fuck away from my table." She started to flush and looked a little sickly. "Now I guess your feelings are hurt," he said. "You've hurt mine too—by bringing your ass over here." The woman just stood there. She didn't know what to do. Pryor continued, "Your next step is to cry and rush to the bathroom." And she did.

He turned to me, Mr. Charming again, and said, "You know, pretty white women like that think they can have anybody, just by being pretty and white. She had no respect for you, but I wanted her to know that I respect black women."

To this day I feel ambivalent about Pryor's behavior that evening. I admired his defense of the dignity of black women—but wondered about his respect for the dignity of all women.

Having traveled to every major metropolitan area of this country, I find fewer nonwhite employees in television stations than at any time since the first wave of guilt-and-fear hiring policies following the riots of the late sixties.

HAYES:

I smile every time I see Max Robinson on ABC's *World News Tonight*. He is the first, the one and the only black nightly anchorperson on a television network in this country. However, at the same time that Max Robinson provides a wonderful (nonathletic) role model for my children, he is also a reminder of how much my industry has failed to provide job opportunities and promotions for nonwhite Americans. Television station managers satisfy government pressure to hire minorities by placing blacks in the mail room. While some minorities can be found in sales and management positions, you have to look real hard to find them. In many stations, you won't find them at all. Tokenism still lives.

There are over 700 television stations in the United States. Two are headed by black station managers. There are three nonwhite program directors; there appear to be fewer and fewer minority union members among the thousands of technicians (mostly men) who work behind the scenes of the glamorous, lucrative and influential television industry.

So when I see Max Robinson, I smile. But I also wonder how many "brothers and sisters" are deciding what stories he reads, or making budget decisions for the ABC *World News Tonight* or contributing to what programs we'll see on prime-time television next season—programs that will be offered for viewing to me and to Max and, much more importantly, to Robert and Toi, my children.

Sheri Singer, a producer of our show, is the third member of the female troika that makes most of the creative decisions regarding the *Donahue* program. Sheri joined our staff after our 1974 move to Chicago. She graduated from high school at 16 and enrolled at the University of Oklahoma. Norman, Oklahoma, turned out to be exactly the escape she was looking for. In high school, she had constantly fought the battle against being characterized as another Jewish American Princess. From the time her parents fulfilled their "great American dream" and moved from Chicago to the North Shore suburb of Skokie, she felt out of place and uncomfortable. As a teen-ager, she had negative perceptions of Skokie—she thought the kids there were very cliquish and snobby. Her decision to go to college in the heart of "Baptist Country" was an attempt to experience a completely different lifestyle.

While an unpaid student employee of KOCO-TV in Oklahoma City, Sheri covered a visit by Presidential candidate George McGovern. With all the enthusiasm of a cub reporter, she got her interview, wrote her script and edited her film. When she sat back that evening to watch herself, she was stunned to see only McGovern's part in the interview—nothing of herself. The next day, the news director said he had cut her out of the piece because she "sounded too Northern and too Jewish." Her broadcasting career in Oklahoma had come to an end, and because of her anger, so did her self-bigotry.

After graduation, Sheri returned to Chicago and worked as news writer/producer at both the ABC and NBC stations there before joining the *Donahue* staff at the ripe old age of 22.

SINGER:

Getting used to working on *Donahue* was a longer and more difficult process than I had imagined. There were seven other people on the staff when I started (that number has since doubled). I had never been faced with a situation like that: Dick and Pat had been with the show since the beginning, eight years before, and Darlene had been the first new addition, two years later. The production staff was like a family, and I was a "newborn" member. I was scared! And I wanted everyone to like me.

I started producing shows almost immediately, but it took several months before I really got the hang of which issues and people would work well in our format. My initial experience with a public relations firm (an occasional source of program ideas) came during my first week. An enthusiastic account executive pitched an enthusiastic associate producer her idea: a representative from Samsonite luggage would demonstrate how to pack for all occasions—family travel, business travel and even emergencies. In my mind I was still producing three-minute segments for television newscasts. This seemed perfect. Pat and Darlene tactfully reminded me that *Donahue* was an hour long, and that packing could be only a short segment. When I got home that night, I realized how foolish the program idea had been. I was sure they had labeled me as one big mistake! But, I did learn early how persuasive someone can be when promoting his or her client. And I finally did learn what kinds of ideas were good for an hour.

One of those we now call the "baby show." Dr. Mayer Eisenstein looks like the man my mother always wanted me to marry—about six feet tall, thick black hair, well built and wearing a white doctor's coat. I liked him the minute I saw him. He is one of the few obstetricians in Chicago who will deliver babies at home. When I told him *Donahue* wanted to videotape the home birth experience, he said he'd inquire whether any of his patients would agree to the presence of a television camera. A short time later he notified me that a couple who lived in a Near North Side Chicago apartment were enthusiastic about the idea. Like a growing number of young couples, they did not like the bureaucratic OB routine of many of today's modern hospitals and saw the *Donahue* program as a chance to evangelize for home delivery.

At 3:30 one afternoon, Dr. Eisenstein called to say, "It looks like it'll be sometime in the next twenty-four hours." I alerted the TV crew and went to sleep that night fully clothed. At 2:45 A.M. my phone rang. I arrived at the apartment of Karen and Al at 3:20 A.M.; the crew came about ten minutes later.

Karen, who was not in any discomfort, sat at the dining-room table drinking coffee, along with her husband, the doctor and a family friend. Her two other children, ages 11 and 4, were sleeping. The crew quietly set up the camera and one dim light as unobtrusively as possible. This wasn't just another news story. A woman was preparing to bring a life into the world.

At 5 A.M. Dr. Eisenstein (whom I was now addressing as "Mayer") advised everyone to get some sleep. His patient would not be delivering for "several hours." There were people sleeping all over the apartment: Karen and Al on the bed in the living room, their friend in one of the boys' rooms; Dr. Eisenstein went to sleep on the floor of a bedroom, and I was on the bed trying to sleep. I could hear Don (the cameraman), Ray (sound) and Al (lighting) chatting and drinking coffee in the dining room. I remember feeling very special. I knew this was an experience I would probably have only once. We were a houseful of strangers living like a family.

Although it was Karen's third child, labor was progressing very slowly. I felt like an expectant father, calling the office every couple of hours with progress reports. I left the house only twice in the fifteen hours I spent there. The first time I went to eat breakfast with the crew. We carefully chose a place within running distance of the apartment. We stayed only about forty-five minutes.

The second time I left the house was at 3:45 that afternoon. I went to a neighborhood deli to get some fruit and soda. When I returned fifteen minutes later, Karen had moved into the final stages of labor. I couldn't believe it. I would have driven my car into the Chicago River if I had missed it! In the "delivery room" with her were the doctor, her 4-year-old son (the older boy had gotten tired of waiting and gone outside to play), her best friend, a physician's assistant, our cameraman and our light man. Her husband was sitting against the back of the sofa bed. His legs were spread so that Karen could sit right up against him, for total physical and emotional support. Al had been rather quiet throughout the experience, but it was easy to see the love and support he now offered his wife. Handel's *Water Music* was softly playing, and Karen was beginning to moan. At this point, I was in another room watching the TV monitor, in headset communication with the cameraman; although I wanted to be right there, I knew it was better to have fewer people in that small room. This way I was able to communicate with Don to make sure he was shooting it the way Phil and I had discussed. The audio engineer was next to me running the equipment.

It was now 4:15 and Karen was moaning loudly. Her nightgown was pulled all the way up, and Al was helping her keep her legs apart. There are no stirrups at home. As the breathing came faster and louder, I felt a knot in my stomach. I was trying to produce a television program, and this brave woman was about to bring a baby into the world without pain-killers of any kind. Dr. Eisenstein was coaching Karen, telling her she was doing beautifully and that it wouldn't be long now. His assistant, Kay, was reminding her to breathe deeply and to push with each contraction. Al was mopping her forehead. All of a sudden I was scared to death. What would happen if something was wrong with the baby? Suddenly, Karen gave a loud, hard push and I saw a round, dark mass start to emerge from the vaginal canal. The head had presented. I somehow maintained contact with Don, describing the shots I wanted, but it was as if I were on Automatic Pilot. I felt a rush of incredible warmth, as Karen reached down to touch the head. Her 4-year-old, who had been watching and asking his mommy questions for the past twenty minutes, cried, "Oh, Mommy, it's a puppy!" Everyone, including Karen, started to laugh in the middle of this intense experience. But it was time to push the head completely out. With one strong grunt and push, the head popped out. It was huge, I thought. Karen laughed and cried at that moment, but there was no time to rest. The body needed to come out now. This took several minutes, and I became worried. Dr. Eisenstein hadn't touched Karen yet, and he said if it took much longer, he would have to help out. Karen was exhausted by now, but she still had work to do. Everyone in the room was coaxing her. I don't know how Don kept the camera steady, but he and the whole crew did a hell of a job.

With a final scream (which still wasn't as bad as in the movies) the baby was out of Karen's body. We all cried out in joy as Dr. Eisenstein said, "It's a girl!" It was exactly 4:27 P.M. Mayer said, "God bless you." Handel's music was still playing. I ran into the room, feeling like a part of Karen, and wanting to be with her as she, Al and their son held Carrie for the first time. The doctor weighed her, and we all howled as the scale tipped 10 pounds! Our camera was still rolling. As soon as the cord stopped pulsating, Dr. Eisenstein cut it. I must admit, I did not watch the placenta being delivered. But I didn't miss anything else. I felt a euphoria that I couldn't remember ever feeling before. I had a new understanding of what it meant to be a woman.

Next, Karen got up and walked to a chair to start nursing Carrie. I could not believe she was actually walking, but Dr. Eisenstein said it was important to nurse the baby in the first hour of life. Al and her son were standing close by as Karen got ready to feed the baby. Then Al was ready with a bottle of champagne, and we all toasted the brave mommy and the new little girl. It was hard for me to realize that ten minutes earlier the little life had been inside Karen's body.

I also experienced something very strange. All of my life I had been scared to death to have a baby, to the point of having two or three nightmares a year about giving birth. I have not had one nightmare since that day.

Totally fascinating was the presence of their 4-year-old son. The little boy was so natural about the birth of his sister. I am sure we all underestimate what a child can handle. I thought this was the best education he would ever get about sex, life and love. And I looked forward to other families across the country being able to experience this through the miracle of television.

Phil and I spent sixteen hours editing the tape. When we finished, I was prouder of it than of anything else I had ever done. The show was scheduled to air on November 4, 1977. I was very excited. I *knew* the show was beautiful and natural. Unfortunately, the men who decide what gets on the air at WGN-TV did not agree. They refused to air the program. I couldn't believe it.

Not only did they refuse to "clear" the show, they refused to tell me why. Dick and Phil were out of town, and the station executives explained that they would discuss it with them when they returned. I couldn't have been more insulted and more angry. Later they told Dick and Phil the "vaginal exposure was too graphic" and that many parents would object to the material airing right before the *Bozo* show, which follows *Donahue* at 12 noon on Channel 9.

Later a compromise was reached, and the WGN management agreed to air the program at 9 o'clock on a Saturday night. The station did not promote the show and almost nobody in Chicago saw it.

The "baby show" taught me a lot about some of the men who make decisions in America's television stations. It taught me about their insecurities, their fears and their failure to understand the maturity of the audience they think they have to "protect."

And the "baby show" also taught me a lot about myself. Working with Phil Donahue has been one of the most growthful experiences in my life, both personally and professionally. I'm not sure I can separate the two. One of the most important lessons I continue to learn is that *nothing is impossible*. Laziness is definitely not one of Phil's traits. If it is necessary to get on a plane at 6 P.M., fly to Washington, D.C., tape a show and return that evening in order to get up and do another live show in Chicago at 11 o'clock the next morning, he'll say, "Let's do it!" And that decision may be made as late as the same afternoon.

If it means running across town at 10:20 A.M. to get a recording of Jim Jones's voice at the time of the Guyana massacre to use during a live 11 A.M. show—"Let's do it!"

If it means bringing a list of statistics that will enhance a show to be put on the electronic computer that prepares visual information for the screen ten minutes before air, or even during a show, Phil still says "Let's do it!"

There are highlights from every *Donahue* show.

Having Burt Reynolds on the program in 1975 before an audience of two hundred women was as wild as a Beatles concert ten years earlier. The women stormed the stage and tore at Reynolds. He finally ripped the emblem off his sweater and gave it to a fan.

John T. Molloy, author of *Dress for Success*, reviewed the wardrobes of the entire *Donahue* production staff. We all failed miserably!

When feminist Susan Brownmiller, known for her book on rape, *Against Our Will*, appeared with Eldridge Cleaver, an admitted rapist, the audience favored Cleaver. They thought

Brownmiller was a "hard woman—one of those hostile Women's Libbers." Susan cried.

When Ann Landers was scheduled on a remote in Milwaukee, a suite was reserved for her use before the taping. I escorted Ms. Landers to her hotel room, but when she opened the door, an elderly lady screamed from the bed. Ann spent the next fifteen minutes consoling me and assuring me it was the hotel's fault.

Ron Weiner became the director of our show when we moved to Chicago. I brought along my own staff, but WGN was providing a studio, the technical crew and the director.

WEINER:

As a television director, I consider myself atypical. I have worked for one department in one station my entire career. As other production people moved from station to station in their search for success, I found that I was upwardly mobile enough within WGN Television to satisfy my need to grow. I have always told my friends and family that "I've never had a day that I didn't want to go to work." I'm not sure I felt that way the day I met Phil and Dick.

The *Donahue* people were using the little conference room along the executive corridor. As I approached for my interview, I squared my shoulders and realized I was nervous. My face felt tight. I knew I was taking things too seriously, but I couldn't get over the feeling that this was a momentous development in my life. I conjured up what I believed would be an intelligent, positive look in my eyes, stepped through the door and—nobody was there!

As if they had been walking in my shadow, Phil and Dick Mincer came through the door. Deadpanned, grim even, it seemed to me. All they said was hello. Talk to them, dummy, I told myself. They've got to be as uptight about you as you are about them. They've got to hold you at arm's length and check you out. But somebody had better say something. I took the initiative, but what came out was something like "Look-I-want-you-to-know-this-is-a-marvelous-opportunity-for-me-I-think-I-can-do-your-show-the-way-you-want-it-but-I'm-supposed-to-be-on-duty-upstairs-now-so-I'll-see-you-later-okay?"

I ran out the door, knowing I'd screwed it up.

Five and a half years, over 1,200 shows and an Emmy Award later, I still don't know what they really thought of me as I fled that first meeting. And I don't want to.

During the show I'm always in a control booth overlooking the studio. I'm the only one on the staff whose view of every *Donahue* show is always received electronically.

Donahue is ad-libbed and off-the-cuff. Since our programs are as varied as fingerprints, our crew has to be especially quick to react to changing situations. The stage is not always our focal point; our studio audiences are more important to me than the millions watching at home. They must be able to see and hear and feel everything that happens. A woman in any one of the studio seats may suddenly be the key person in a particular show. We hang on her expression and her every word. She is vital to us. That's what makes *Donahue* unique.

Our show is often done before live audiences in other cities around the country. Unlike the WGN crew, the technicians in cities we visit are not prepared to operate with either Phil or me. I talk with them at length before the remote begins, explaining to each one what I expect him or her to do. They go into the week thinking they can handle it. They come out of the week wanting another shot at it.

When the show begins, the crowd's reaction to Phil's entrance is loud, warm, thrilling. Three or four or five thousand people are applauding, cheering, screaming with excitement. I call the cameras around to cover his walk to the stage, then whip them back to crowd shots. My voice barks at them: "Wider, pan, take Three, tighten up, take One, zoom out, hurry up, Camera Four give me Phil tight, Two get wide, wider, take Two, music in, ride that applause, higher, start the playback tape, take it!"

I remember my first trip with the show. It was to Niagara Falls in late spring, 1974. It was the first time I'd ever worked with a crew I didn't know and I was apprehensive. But everything fell into place; the results were gratifying, and there were some great comic moments: Mr. Blackwell, creator of the infamous "worst-dressed" list, gave a lady a hat he'd designed and while Phil was placing it on her head he accidentally knocked off her wig; Cleveland Amory brought a large brown bear that fell asleep backstage and missed his cue; Phil was able to make another animal pay off as he rode an elephant onstage in the glare of the spotlights for a closing shot I'll never forget.

Late one afternoon Phil and I went to see the falls. I stood behind a slat-and-wire fence about 30 yards back of a promontory, but Phil was out beyond the fence, leaning over the railing at the edge to look into the churning water. He waved me over. The fence between us was leaning away from me, so it was easy for me to clamber over it to join him.

We were totally absorbed by the sight and sound. I wondered why the park authorities hadn't removed the snow fence—it was nearly summer. "That's not a snow fence," Phil said, matter-of-factly. "That's to keep people away from here. This piece of cliff may drop into the river."

"See you later," I said, backing toward the fence.

"Not that way," said Phil. "The fence is slanting toward us. We'll never get over it. Let's go this way." He sauntered to the railing at the side of the condemned point of land. Oblivious to the mile-a-minute torrent just beneath his feet, he threw one leg at a time over the rail and, with his back and buttocks swung out over the foam, inched his way around the end of the slat fence. "Your turn," he said as he hopped on to safe ground.

It was getting darker. I felt cold, and I could see the headline in the morning paper: FALLS CLAIM 96TH VICTIM!

"Come on," called Donahue. "Nothing to it." I made it, but I shudder just remembering.

After the fourth show in Niagara Falls, the staff was invited to a cocktail party which honored the finalists of that year's Miss U.S.A. contest. On an emotional high because the show had gone so well, and very full of myself and of three or four bloody Marys, I mingled with the beauty queens, show folk and local V.I.P.s. I felt so terrific I needed to share my ebullience with my wife. I called Phyllis at home in Highland Park.

Her "Hello" was like a wail, but I didn't notice.

"You'll never guess what, Phyl," I babbled. "The Miss U.S.A. thing is here and I'm at a party with the winners. Are they beautiful! I think Miss Oregon will win it, but Miss Illinois is terrific too!"

Of course I couldn't see that her jeans were rolled up to her knees, that her hair was hanging in her face and that she had a wet mop in her hand. But I could hear her. "Well, goody for you! It's been raining here all day, and the basement's flooded!" *Click!*

The party just wasn't the same after that.

My most difficult remote was from aboard the *Delta Queen* on the Ohio River in 1975. Dick Mincer and I boarded her a month before to work out logistics. We picked places for staging guests and musical numbers and selected the laundry area as our control room. There was heavy equipment in the next compartment—the spare generator—but we were told it was never used since the regular generators were the most dependable on the river.

By remote week, the Ohio was at flood stage. There was a lengthy delay because we had to move people and equipment to meet the *Queen* at Madison, Indiana, instead of Cincinnati, but we felt that if we hurried we could set up in time to tape a segment with the Stephen Foster Singers before the sun set.

We got shots of Phil on the gangplank in antebellum costume, with some of the fashion-show models in hoopskirts and pantaloons and the people of Madison waving from the bank. It was charming. As the boat churned downriver, we placed the choir on the ship's bridge and along the railings and taped three of their songs. The boat was steaming into the wind, flags flying; "My Old Kentucky Home" filled the air. The sun was sinking into the horizon ahead of us. Lovely!

To make up for the time we'd lost, we decided to try a couple of segments more. We set up lights, plugged them in and started the tape rolling. After about two minutes, the lights went out, the equipment went off and Phil, Dick and I went through the roof. Also, the *Delta Queen*'s paddle wheel went dead. We sat there, drifting down the river, knowing we'd gone too far: we'd overloaded the boat's electrical system.

When we'd planned the cruise, there had been no thought of night taping. So when we plugged in all the lights, all the cameras, all the tape machines, all the consoles and switching machines and audio equipment at the same time—that's when "the most dependable generators on the river" decided to call it quits.

The spare generator in the room next to our control room roared into life and we were back in business. One problem: I had to shout my cues above the sound of the machinery. It was loud. Deafeningly loud.

In the next forty-eight hours we completed four shows, and we needed those lights all the time, because the sun, which had gone down so magnificently that first evening, seemed to have gone down for good. For two days we had nothing but overcast and fog—so dense we couldn't even see the riverbank. Shouting over the roar of the generator, my voice grew more and more hoarse.

At the end of our second full day, I could not speak above a whisper. "Dick," I rasped, "I can't go on."

"What?"

"I said I can't go on. You'll have to direct the last show."

"What?"

"The crew can't hear me over the cue system!"

Dick looked at me thoughtfully. "I can't hear what the hell you're saying, Ron, and nobody else can either, so I'll direct the last show."

Next morning the sun came out, beautiful and brilliant. Green trees on the banks, cattle grazing as we glided by, kids waving (one was even rolling a hoop along the top of the levee, for pity's sake) and the *Delta Queen* paddling along in a living picture postcard.

As I watched Dick weave those gorgeous scenes into that last show, my heart was breaking. I'd waited the whole trip for shots like these. Now that they were available, I was unable to say even, "Fade up Camera One." I did the only thing I could. I kneed him in the kidneys—hard. "Son of a bitch!" I croaked.

Dick looked back over his shoulder at me. "What do you want now?"

"The sun, dammit, the sun!!"

"Well, you should have *told* me you wanted sun. I wanted sun, so I got sun. After all, I'm the executive producer. It's my job to arrange things like that. Why are you crying? . . ."

Here are a couple of times I laughed instead of cried.

Farrah Fawcett spent over an hour in the dressing room with a makeup artist and hairstylist, then told a Los Angeles studio audience, "My hair? Oh, I just sort of toss it around up there and that's how it comes out."

Milton Berle, who'd been our guest, and the rest of us were flying back to Chicago from a remote in Detroit. The plane was delayed on the ground. After we'd sat there for half an hour, Uncle Miltie walked to the flight attendant's station, picked up the microphone and did a half-hour of oneliners for the benefit of the passengers. Talk about captive audiences!

The first person we hired when we moved to Chicago was Penny Rotheiser. As manager, press relations, she arranges for newspapers, magazines and other talk-show hosts to interview me, promotes the program and in general tries her best to make me look good. One of the questions she is most commonly asked is how she got into this field.

ROTHEISER:

The media has always fascinated me—and still does. I guess I knew as far back as the third grade, when I helped start a news-paper, that I had to be involved in this field. My parents en-couraged me to pursue my journalistic goals, but also felt obliged to suggest I "get a degree in education to fall back on," as so many of the girls I grew up with in suburban Chicago did in those days. I didn't.

After receiving a degree in journalism, with a radio-TV major, from the University of Missouri, I set out to become "Mary Tyler Rotheiser." I spent the next few years helping produce TV shows at a Chicago station, and later I handled public relations for two nightclubs.

In 1974, I read an item in a *Chicago Tribune* column about a nationally syndicated show moving to WGN-TV. Phil Donahue was bringing his Dayton-based talk show to Chicago. I began making phone calls and tracked down Dick Mincer, who asked if I had ever done public relations. I put on my best suit, grabbed my portfolio and went off to an interview that turned out to have more of an effect on my life than I had ever imagined.

After three years of working as promotion manager—servicing the constantly growing number of stations carrying the program, creating promos (on-air spots) and handling the publicity—I be-came Phil's press manager and zeroed in on obtaining national press coverage. *The Saturday Evening Post* had already done a profile, and *Good Housekeeping* had been the first of the "women's magazines" to feature Phil. But generally, though the number of viewers was rapidly increasing, we weren't getting much attention from the media. Some newspaper columnists had been supportive, but as I pursued magazine editors in New York, I heard a lot of "Dona-who?" Until the show became number one on WNBC-TV.

With one Emmy under our belt (to Phil as "best host") and this newfound recognition, I went to New York for a week, complete with press kits, ratings, story ideas—and just about everything but Phil's baby picture—to meet with editors about possible articles. I talked with *Redbook, Parade, Newsweek, Us, Family Circle,* United Press International, Associated Press, the New York *Daily News* and so on until I was lunch-dinner-and-cocktailed into a new dress size. Most of the people were receptive to the idea of doing a story on this new "overnight sensation," as I kept hearing the editors call Phil. It didn't matter that he had a strong background as a newsman, or that the *Donahue* show by then had already been on the air over ten years. What mattered was that New York had discovered Phil Donahue—he was now their "fair-haired boy," and about to experience "the New York hype."

The past two years have been a hectic schedule of deciding who gets to talk to Phil, when and where. And my job has become a juggling act. As soon as I confirm long-nurtured plans for a *Newsweek* cover story, *Time* calls. And *People. Redbook, Good Housekeeping, Ladies' Home Journal, Family Circle* and *Lady's Circle* all call within two weeks. Writers preparing stories on everything from the celebrity's favorite recipes to the Equal Rights Amendment call to get Phil's comments. And a day rarely goes by without a newspaper TV editor, radio- or TV-show host, gossip columnist or college student calling to request an interview.

I've accompanied Phil on press trips, helped photographers lug around cumbersome camera equipment, stuffed press releases into envelopes at midnight, arranged press conferences and updated Phil's biography nine times. Articles have appeared in *Newsweek, Esquire, Reader's Digest, Redbook, Ladies' Home Journal, McCall's, People, TV Guide, Broadcasting, Family Weekly* and many other publications. And it feels good to know I've been a part of it all.

Of course, there have been some frustrating experiences. After much coaxing, *Us* magazine decided to accompany the *Donahue* show on the 1977 remote aboard the *Mississippi Queen* (sister ship of the *Delta Queen*). A photographer was to stay with us a few days to shoot material for a profile on Phil. I went to New Orleans (where we were to board the ship) one day early to work out press logistics. I met with the ship's P.R. director, and we spent the rest of the day planning who would cover what—and how.

My contact at *Us* called. "We've decided not to come on the remote—we've just found out Marlo Thomas is going to be on next week's cover of *People* magazine." I told him the story coming out on Marlo had absolutely nothing to do with Phil. It would mention him incidentally, but the story was on Marlo—to promote her upcoming Christmas special. I again explained how *Us* would have a fresh story that no other magazine would have. "Just the same, I think we'll pass, and if there really isn't a conflict, we'll call you back in Chicago and arrange something then."

Four months later, *Us* assigned a Chicago reporter to do a profile on Phil. They needed the material in a hurry, so I set up interview sessions and rushed the necessary photos to them. Then the writer called and said he had been told to rewrite the story—the editor wanted more about Phil and Marlo's relationship. The writer added more material, and we waited to hear when it would be scheduled. After months of communication with *Us*, I learned from an editor that they had killed the story because it wasn't fresh!

Phil is a very private person, and I have the ever-present challenge of guarding that privacy, while still getting publicity. And sometimes he doesn't realize his own appeal. After one year of negotiations with *People* magazine, convincing them why their readers would be interested in reading about him, I had to persuade Phil to let them do the story. He looked up and said, "Why would *People* want to do a story on me?"

Some of the humorous, tedious or touching moments I won't forget:

Dining at the Governor's mansion in Atlanta with Phil and the staff during a remote week there.

The numerous appearances on *Donahue* during "letter shows."

The royal welcome we received in Huntington, West Virginia, complete with two limousines, chilled champagne in ice buckets, a police escort through town, a sign larger than my bedroom welcoming us to town—and losing my luggage.

A photographer getting an aerial shot of the *Delta Queen* during our remote by hanging out of the Goodyear blimp. And Phil, angered by the noise it was creating, having to stop the show and signal him to go away. And the photographer thinking Phil was just waving hello to him.

Phil and me lying on WGN's snow-covered lawn and flapping our arms and legs back and forth to make angels during one of Chicago's storms.

Running out of gas on the San Diego Freeway on the way to the first show of a remote. And being rescued by a truck driver with a C.B., who used it to reach a highway patrol service that gave me fuel.

After six months of discussions, getting Phil on the cover of *TV Guide*.

Having to throw out almost all the clothes and shoes I had worn during a remote at the Ohio State Fair because they had been ruined by the mud and rain.

Sitting on the office floor with other staff members surrounding Phil as he heard his name announced on TV as the winner of his first national Emmy.

A press conference in San Francisco where Phil, tired from a busy interview schedule, introduced me as "the woman traveling with me."

The time we featured Wayne Dyer as a guest, talking about his book *Your Erroneous Zones,* and WGN used a "This show is intended for adult viewing" disclaimer. They thought we were discussing erogenous zones.

The evening Phil signed Merv Griffin's name to an autograph because that's who the person requesting one thought he was.

Shlepping press kits—Everywhere.

Not many men are heroes to their secretaries. I happen to be one of the lucky ones—lucky because Lorraine Landelius is my secretary.

LANDELIUS:

Where have the last five years gone? Have they been glamorous, exciting? Decide for yourself.

At 45, after raising a family of four, I wanted to enrich my life. I decided to go to college to see if I had missed anything. I also joined the army of temporary help, working as a Kelly Girl for five years. The assignments were varied—from sporting-goods order billing to office vacation replacement to a wide variety of secretarial jobs at WGN. I had no desire for a full-time job until I received a call from Dick Mincer asking me to come in for an interview—the *Donahue* show needed a secretary. I took the job that millions of women in America envy. And what a job it's turned out to be! The duties are as varied as any secretary's would be—and that's only where they start.

Most mornings Phil comes in, suit slung over his shoulder, and jokingly announces to one and all, "Star's here!" That's the only predictable part of my day.

All day, somewhere in the United States, people are watching *Donahue*, and they call our office to express their opinions or get the address of the day's guest. Sandwiched between the mountains of daily mail (all letters must be answered) and the never-ending succession of phone calls are a few much more interesting tasks. For example—I have discussed characteristics of handwriting with Nobel Prize-winning economist Milton Friedman, chatted with actor Alan Alda about his daughters, exchanged child-rearing theories with Dr. Spock, ironed Betty Ford's dress and zipped up gowns on models for the world's most famous designers. I've appeared on TV with the secretaries of Marlon Brando, John Denver and John Travolta. Billy Carter has kissed me, and Beverly Sassoon and I have discussed our current college classes. I went to a baseball game with Henry Winkler's mother, and I've actually been on the diamond at Wrigley Field to help interview the Cubs' home-run leader, Dave Kingman.

Like all of the production assistants, I have to be ready for any emergency. However, none of us was ready for a freak snowstorm in April, 1975. It was impossible to get home. The staff was marooned at the station—warm, but thirsty. Adventurous Phil borrowed a hat, a jacket, boots and a sled from the prop department and plowed his way to a local tavern for beer. But all he had with him was a checkbook. Smiling at the bartender and the few other patrons who had braved the storm, he asked "Does anyone here know me?"

Phil believes that his program is a product of the entire staff. We depend on each other. He considers the office staff and our families as his "family." Last year my husband, George, was hospitalized in Phoenix. At that time Phil was participating in the John Denver Annual Ski Tournament in Colorado. He broke away from his busy schedule to phone George: "I just skied with John Denver. It's great here." Phil wanted George to share in his enthusiasm, knowing that George is a fan of Denver and that we love Colorado.

I can always tell where Phil is on an out-of-town trip from the phone calls from fans that say, "Mr. Donahue said to call for tickets." Phil never shrugs off requests for tickets or pictures. He just says, "Call Lorraine."

Occasionally a caller will ask "Are you *just* the secretary?" Definitely not. I have my fans too. On a recent vacation in Hawaii (compliments of "the boss"), a man approached me. "You're Phil Donahue's secretary. I saw you on television. May I have your autograph?"

And now let's give Pat McMillen the final word and let's hope she's speaking for all the staff.

McMILLEN:

Our jobs are probably more glamorous than most jobs people have. There are premiere parties you get invited to that other people only dream about or see in the movies. We fly around the country to work, and we meet and work with exciting, interesting and glamorous people. The job certainly never gets dull or boring. In fact, we have talked many times in the office about the pace and the excitement level and wondered what would happen if we were ever to do anything else not quite so demanding. We'd probably all be bored to death.

However, for all those people who think television is the ideal, glamorous and ultimate job, it is also important to note that television offers no security whatever. You're here today and gone tomorrow. People are working purely with creative ideas and concepts, and if someone comes up with a better idea than yours, your idea is out, at whatever expense to your ego. It is extremely competitive, not only in terms of other shows getting better ratings, but also in the way personalities react to each other.

The *Donahue* show has a far better employment record than other TV shows. The same three—Phil, Dick and I—are still together after twelve years. Darlene, the first person to join our staff, is still with us after ten years, and I hope that all those who have ever been a part of the *Donahue* staff will continue to feel the importance of their contribution.

14

TV Bosses

THE MEN who manage America's seven-hundred-plus television stations are almost always models of the American success story. In most cases, they preside over enterprises that make money even when badly managed. Although inflation, proliferation of television channels and a growing cable system have made competition more intense, a television license is still a voucher worth a good deal of cash.

To ensure the renewal of the station's license every three years, television general managers—usually vice-presidents of their companies—hire "community affairs" directors, whose job is to determine which local do-gooders receive free public-service air time. Community service directors can usually be found at lunch with members of various "minorities" or the head of Goodwill Industries or the local Army recruiter. Their biggest responsibility is to see that the renewal application is a thick, well-documented account of all that the station has done to "determine the community interests" and what was done to fulfill them. All public-service programs (most of which air on Sunday mornings or in other low-revenue times) are exhaustively detailed.

The TV general manager is almost always a member of the local opera or symphony board (meetings of which are often attended by his community affairs director). Other noncontroversial civic activities, such as the United Appeal, receive immediate and enthusiastic backing and free air time by general managers anxious to place this example of community involvement in their license-renewal files.

General managers are also four-square in favor of "Toys for Tots,"

"Neediest Children's Funds" at Christmas, Yom Kippur greetings "to our Jewish friends" on station breaks and editorials urging citizen support of Girl Scout cookies, volunteer firemen and the dedicated people of the Civil Air Patrol.

Somewhere in the halls of the understaffed, overworked and bureaucratic Federal Communications Commission, is there really a person who reads these fat dossiers of virtue and generosity? It is a good question, because thousands of hours and thousands of dollars are spent every year on this mandatory horn blowing.

It is the feudal homage of general managers to the lordly Federal Government, pleading: "Please don't pull my license!" Someday I *may* understand their anxiety. However, in all the years of commercial broadcasting, only a handful of licenses have not been renewed.

To be sure, recent challenges of license renewals have been vigorous and, in some few cases, have provided bona fide reasons for general-manager jitters. Women, blacks and other minorities are becoming more vocal and more effective in protesting what they feel are discriminatory hiring practices and program policies. In spite of the increase in the volume and frequency of these protests, however, broadcasting's status quo is hardly in danger. This is because the FCC appointees are often friends of the industry they are supposed to regulate (nothing new for regulatory agencies). Not infrequently, they exchange one hat for another. For instance, former Commissioner Lee Loevinger, following his term on the FCC, joined the Washington law firm that represented the late Avco Broadcasting Corporation, to name just one example.

Most television general managers enjoy community prestige. They have glamorous, high-visibility jobs and enjoy discussing their on-air personalities at cocktail parties. They will regale neighbors with inside stories about their most popular local celebrities. Most TV general managers call rabbis by their first names, have kids who play tennis, belong to a country club and know how to kick ass when salesmen fail to meet monthly quotas. Most, to their credit, stay out of their news departments, but many television news people are able to relate at least one off-the-record incident of having to kill a story that would have embarrassed an important local sponsor.

Some general managers preside over an immensely lucrative "bottom line" but will deny small pay raises to loyal employees or turn thumbs down on T-shirts for the girls' softball team while authorizing thousands of dollars to televise a local golf tournament even though the only people interested are the golfers who are on the course.

54. Senator Edward Kennedy—January 27, 1977.

55. Rosalynn Carter—May 16, 1979.

56. Frank Collin, President of the National Socialist Party of America (Neo-Nazi Party), and David Duke, National Director of the Ku Klux Klan—July 7, 1978.

57. Albert Speer, Hitler's architect and Minister of Armaments and War Production —Heidelberg, Germany, October 30, 1975.

58. The Reverend Jesse Jackson—January 12, 1977.

59. The Reverend Billy Graham—October 11, 1979.

60. Gregory Peck—June 17, 1976.

61. Farrah Fawcett—Los Angeles, August 8, 1978.

62. Burt Reynolds—May 23, 1978.

63. John Wayne—April 26, 1976.

64. Henry Fonda—March 30, 1979.

65. Dolly Parton—April 29, 1977.

66. Sammy Davis, Jr.—July 24, 1978.

67. My dog, Tida, and Lassie— March 5, 1976.

68. Playing piano with Liberace— November 25, 1976.

69. Pete Rose—Cincinnati's River- front Coliseum, August 3, 1978.

70. Football with Alice Cooper—
April 1, 1975.

71. Tennis with Bill Cosby—July
14, 1975.

72. Boxing with "The Champ,"
Muhammad Ali—October 26,
1977.

Television executives, like talk-show hosts, also come in assorted ego sizes. Some are the boss, some are the President, some are like emperors and a few are called by God.

John T. Murphy was my boss's boss's boss. Mr. Murphy had the earthly title of president of the Avco Broadcasting Corporation. And you better damn well believe it. Mr. Murphy had a nasty habit of humiliating his vice-presidents in front of all his other vice-presidents. He was the archetypal example of one man's power over another's livelihood. It was power that turned frightened mortgage-holding underlings into scampering yes-men. In more than one meeting, Murphy interrupted a nervously delivered opinion with the words "You can speak English better than that. I've heard you."

On no other occasion was Mr. Murphy's power more evident than during his annual visits to the four television stations that Avco owned outside its headquarters city of Cincinnati. While "presidential visits" are a sound business idea, in the case of Mr. Murphy they became very costly and time-consuming exercises that had more to do with ego than with good communication.

Following is a portion of an eighteen-page memo written by the station's promotion director, who had the nerve-racking job of overseeing the details of one such annual visit.

TO: Mary Bates, Ray Colie   Date: 12/3/73
FROM: Ron Niess
SUBJECT: WLWD Presidential Visit
cc: Boyce Lancaster

Outlined below is the proposed agenda for WLWD's station visit by Avco Broadcasting President John T. Murphy and other Corporate executives:

TUESDAY, DECEMBER 11, 1973

5:00 P.M.   *Pre-Meeting Arrival*
                    (a) Arrival of Mr. Murphy, Mr. Bartlett and Mrs. Bates at the Mall Motor Inn (21 South Jefferson Street)

                    (b) Mr. George Gray will arrive at Cox Municipal Airport. Arrangements will be made for pick-up and transportation to Mall Motor Inn.

(c) All Corporate guests will be pre-registered, as follows:
Mr. Murphy—Lg. Suite
Mr. Bartlett—Sm. Suite
Mr. Gray—Single
Mrs. Bates—Single
Mr. Anthony—Single
Mr. Colie—Single

(d) Mr. Colie will be in the lobby of the Mall Motor Inn to welcome Mr. Murphy and Corporate guests, and will present each with room key.

(e) Refreshments and flowers will be provided in each guest room.

7:30 P.M.   *Cocktails and Dinner*
(a) Mr. Murphy, Mr. Bartlett, Mr. Gray, Mrs. Bates and Mr. Colie will have dinner together. Actual time, place and mode of transportation to be announced.

(b) In the event Mr. Murphy chooses not to dine together, Mrs. Bates will be hosted at Dinner by Ron Niess and Boyce Lancaster, or be advised otherwise. Time, place and mode of transportation to be announced.

WEDNESDAY, DECEMBER 12, 1973

9:00 A.M.–9:45 A.M.   *Breakfast*
(a) Mr. Colie will join Mr. Murphy, Mr. Bartlett, Mr. Gray, and Mrs. Bates for breakfast

in coffee shop of the Mall
Motor Inn.

9:45 A.M.–10:00 A.M. *Hotel Departure*

(a) Chauffeured limousine will
pick up Mr. Murphy, Mr.
Bartlett, Mr. Gray, Mrs. Bates
and Mr. Colie at Mall Motor
Inn and proceed to the Trailsend Club for scheduled morning activities.

10:00 A.M.–10:15 A.M. *News Interview*

(a) On arrival at the Trailsend
Club, Mr. Murphy will be interviewed by Dick Bay. This
sound-on-film interview will
be conducted in the first floor
library of the Trailsend Club.
NOTE: Questions to be
asked during this in-
terview have been
submitted to Mrs.
Bates.

Luncheon

(a) Hors d'oeuvres will be available in the Gaslight Room preceding lunch.

(b) Lunch will be pre-ordered,
the menu consisting of:
Small Fillet
Oven-Brown potatoes
Vegetable
Salad with choice of dressing
Light dessert (parfait, ice
cream, etc.)

(c) A seating plan for lunch will
indicate where each person
will sit. Name cards will be
on the table.

(d) A photographer has been
scheduled.

1:45 P.M.–2:00 P.M.	*Depart Trailsend Club to WLWD*
	(a) Mr. Murphy, Corporate Executives and Mr. Colie will depart Trailsend Club via limousine to WLWD station.

2:00 P.M.–5:00 P.M.	*General Staff Meeting*
	1) To the left of Mr. Murphy's table between left-side TV monitor and Mr. Murphy's table will be small table. Seated there will be Mrs. Bates and Mickey Leisner. Along with pitchers of water, pencils and paper will be employee service pins and bracelets. During awards presentation, Mr. Murphy will stand slightly to the side of small table, with Mary Bates and Mickey Leisner behind same table. Sufficient light and sound will be provided.
	2) Name cards will be placed in front of each individual seated at Mr. Murphy's table. Likewise at Mrs. Bates' table.

MISCELLANEOUS

A—Suites and single rooms at the Mall Motor Inn will be "stocked" as follows:

    1—Mr. Murphy's and Mr. Bartlett's suites—floral arrangements with welcome note from Mr. Colie and entire WLWD staff; bottle of J & B; bottle of Walker's Deluxe; ice, glasses, etc.

    2—Mr. Gray's and Mrs. Bates' singles—floral arrangement and welcome note from Mr. Colie and WLWD staff; bottle of J & B; ice, glasses, etc.

B—The highway signs at the north and south sides of the WLWD building complex will contain the following message on WEDNESDAY, DECEMBER 12, 1973:

TV 2 WELCOMES
JOHN T. MURPHY

AND
WALTER BARTLETT

C—Department heads and luncheon guests will all wear WLWD name tags.

D—All employees will wear similar name tags throughout the afternoon.

E—Several questions will be pre-planned for the Q & A session and will be used in the event the session should happen to bog down.

F—The entire employee meeting, presentation and Q & A session and service pin ceremony will be audio taped (7½ ips single track).

Ron Niess, Director
Promotion/Publicity
RN:mb

Not only did Mr. Colie, himself a vice-president, have to be in the lobby when Mr. Murphy arrived at the hotel; he was also obliged to have Mr. Murphy's room key in hand to ensure that our president did not have to bother with any time-consuming rigamarole at the check-in desk.

Notice also that Mr. Murphy had a wonderful way of dealing with the media over which he presided. "Questions to be asked during [Mr. Murphy's station] interview have been submitted to Mrs. Bates." No surprises here. An obedient newsman (with a big mortgage and three kids) dutifully delivered the first questions in accordance with the approved list. And the interview was aired on the evening newscast in entirety. No edits.

This man was the last word in one of America's most powerful broadcast groups. He headed a company with five television stations (in Cincinnati, Dayton, Columbus, Indianapolis and San Antonio) and seven radio stations. Literally hundreds of news people worked for him and had the job of finding and reporting news of their various communities. Since the news does not always flatter the people who make it, why should Mr. Murphy have had the privilege of screening questions when politicians and other businessmen must live with the questions they get?

Further, what did this man's total control over his own "news event" do to the professional attitude of the reporters who worked for him? How aggressive could we expect Avco Broadcasting news people to be when questioning other community power brokers if the questions for their own president had to be "submitted to Mrs. Bates" beforehand? It seemed incredible that one of America's most important communications companies was headed by a man who was so totally intimidated by that part of his job which called for him to communicate.

When Mr. Murphy's visit had ended, literally weeks of hard work and thousands of dollars in hard cash had been spent writing, filming and editing the "Station Presentation." While the employees lined up to receive their five-, ten- and fifteen-year employment pins (complete with the smallest diamonds in the history of jewelry), I sat in the back row and longed for a corporation president who spent money on pay raises rather than flattering "Station Presentations" and who would frequently show up at the good ol' "local level"—without the limousines and the personalized marquee—gather the loyal troops in a room, take off his coat, roll up his sleeves and say:

"Hi. I'm your president. Any questions?"

15
Censorship

Avco Broadcasting was the whale that swallowed the Jonah that was once the proud and innovative Crosley Broadcasting Company of Cincinnati. Jonah's name at birth was WLW radio, "50-thousand-watt voice of the Midwest," and it boasted about launching the careers of Andy Williams, Doris Day, Rosemary Clooney and others. Powell Crosley liked local live broadcasting and made his firm one of the few broadcast groups in the country to find, pay for, produce and promote local live programming. (It was a lot easier, and in some ways more lucrative, to air reruns of *I Love Lucy*.) This tradition fortunately continued after the death of Mr. Crosley (who sustained a big business setback with, of all things, a small car; he was only ten years ahead of his time).

To John Murphy's credit, he not only continued the "local live" policy but also, throughout the entire life of our show, never interfered with our efforts to produce an exciting, controversial, adult, tell-it-like-it-is program.

Except once.

Driving from Dayton to Cincinnati takes about an hour. All the way down I-75 in southwestern Ohio, I wondered why I had been summoned to meet with Walter Bartlett, Vice-President for Television, Avco Broadcasting. Throughout the four years we had been on the air, my contact with the management team in Cincinnati had been restricted to the annual presidential visit and a cocktail party at Christmas. Now I was being invited to a meeting with the second-most-powerful man in the corporation. And I had no idea why.

As I sat in Mr. Bartlett's outer office waiting to see him, there was no hint in the small talk his secretary, Gittie, and I carried on that something unpleasant was about to happen. When I finally walked into his office, exchanging the usual banter about Pete Rose and Johnny Bench and the Cincinnati Reds, Mr. Bartlett got right to the point.

"We don't want Nicholas Johnson on your program," he said.

So there it was. Nothing sneaky. No gray here. No big song-and-dance. After four years of no interference, the management team, without any baloney, was censoring my program.

Nicholas Johnson was a member of the Federal Communications Commission. An Iowa liberal, he had been appointed by Lyndon B. Johnson, and although he was no relative, there were scores of broadcasters who insisted that nepotism had to have been the only reason the "son of a bitch" got the job. Broadcasters not only hated Nicholas Johnson: they talked often and seriously about impeaching him. Although the FCC had often been accused of being in bed with the industry it is charged with regulating, Johnson was the exception that proves the rule. He had written a book instructing the public on how to challenge commercial TV licenses, and while the National Association of Broadcasters was accustomed to meeting in the largest hotel in town, Johnson could generally be found in the Holiday Inn across the street telling blacks and other minorities what they were entitled to from the local boob tube. He drove the TV guys crazy.

"We don't want Nicholas Johnson on your program," Mr. Bartlett repeated.

"We," it was clear to me, meant John T. Murphy, a man adamantly opposed to government interference. Murphy was not about to send Johnson on tape out to all the *Donahue* stations for a full hour of antibroadcaster propaganda. I wasn't there when it happened, but I am betting my next rating that when Murphy discovered the booking, he immediately pushed Walter Bartlett's button and laid down "Murphy's Law." And there was nothing funny about Murphy's Law. Failure to obey it could cost you your job, and no single *Donahue* program was worth a person's job.

Except mine.

"Why?" I asked.

"Because we think he is irresponsible and is just trying to make a name for himself and we don't want to give him the platform," Bartlett said.

I said I thought the request was unfair. I volunteered something to the effect that Johnson was a "duly authorized member of the United States Government" and this seemed to be a "blatant example of censorship." Then I gently and nervously (my mortgage at the time was $25,000 and I had five kids) played my trump card. "What if the newspapers should find out about this?" I said.

Now I really had Mr. Bartlett's attention, and it was clear to him that I might not go down as easily as some of the other mortgage holders. At the time, the show was bringing in probably a half-million dollars a year to Avco Broadcasting's gross sales. This didn't make me Sinatra, but I wasn't the weekend weatherman either. I left the office without saying whether I planned to fold or stay in the game.

By the time I got to my car, I knew I couldn't fold. The issue was not even complicated. Nick Johnson was an FCC member, and any attempt to keep him off the program was indefensible. Driving home, I talked to myself out loud.

"Nicholas Johnson is a duly authorized member of the Government of the United States of America (Go, Phil, baby!) and to deny him access to our airwaves would be a gross violation of his right of free speech. Besides, how come you never disallowed critics of other industries from appearing on my program? General Motors would have loved to have the power to keep Ralph Nader off the air. Kellogg's and General Foods would have loved to have censored Robert Choate, who told my audience recently that breakfast cereal has less nutrient value than a shot of booze. How can I criticize other industries when you won't allow me to feature guests who might criticize our own? Indefensible! Immoral! (Applause, applause.) Therefore, I cannot continue to serve as host of a program that only pretends to speak to all sides of issues. I must resign, therefore, from the Avco Broadcasting Company with a heavy but nevertheless pure heart. (Standing applause.) Good night, and may God bless you all."

I looked down at my speedometer and discovered I was going eighty miles an hour.

Several days after I got home and had partly vented my spleen in the preliminary skirmishes, I typed a two-page statement condemning the hypocrisy of advertising *Donahue* as an honest, tell-it-like-it-is program and said:

. . . I am prepared to risk my job with Avco on this issue. If

Avco chooses to disallow Mr. Johnson's appearance on my program at some future date, then I no longer wish to provide my services to the company. . . .

Five minutes after the memo arrived in Cincinnati I was summoned again. All the way on I-75 I thought of my mortgage and my kids.

Inside Bartlett's office he offered me the following solution to my moral dilemma—a solution undoubtedly approved by Mr. Murphy:

I could feature Commissioner Johnson on my program, but not alone. I must also invite Lee Loevinger to appear on the same show. As mentioned earlier, Lee Loevinger was a former member of the FCC and later a Washington lawyer for Avco Broadcasting.

After some hesitation, I agreed. However half-assed, it was a deal, and I accepted. Not a total victory, not a sellout.

When the program finally aired, Commissioner Johnson spoke eloquently (I thought) about the enormous profit the TV industry enjoys and said with conviction that broadcasters do not care about people, they care about money—and lots of it. The result, he said, was the exploitation of not only adults but children as well. Loevinger vigorously countered with facts about high-cost news departments ("They lose money") and offered examples of outstanding television fare like *The Waltons* and various documentaries.

When it was over I felt only half-good. And I continued to meet my mortgage payments.

In 1979, *Donahue* and the NBC *Today* show signed an agreement whereby our office would produce three *Today* segments per week. In case you think the Big Apple is different, one month after the agreement went into effect, a *Donahue* segment was rejected in its entirety: Dr. Brantley Scott, urologist from the Baylor Medical Center in Houston, displaying and explaining a prosthesis, an expandable "penile implant" for male patients who suffer waist-down paralysis. It was banned from the *Today* show because "we don't like to discuss sex at that hour of the morning." Future instructions: "No clinical sex" for the *Today* show segments.

Television stations that carry *Donahue* have every legal right to cancel any program we send them. This feature of TV syndication works as a check and balance against the *Donahue* office in Chicago. We believe all the programs we send out are air worthy, but we also realize that reasonable people can differ on certain kinds of programs. And while some of our shows have been banned in some cities, the point must be made that in almost every case, our programs are cleared by station managers who believe, with us, that television's problem is not controversy, it is blandness. And that the viewing public is far more prepared to accept sensitive subject matter than many of the TV moguls have assumed.

Today, the *Donahue* program enjoys more editorial freedom than any other television production. Our office in Chicago receives no interference from our management team headed by Multimedia Broadcasting's president, Walter Bartlett. The same trust is evident in the supervision of Wilson Wearn, the president of Multimedia, Inc., and the man to whom Bartlett reports. Failing to acknowledge this very positive feature of our creative life would be to ignore one of the most important features of *Donahue*'s success over the past several years.

16
New York

OUR PROGRAM had been alive only three years and was being seen in about seven markets when, lo and behold, WPIX in big, sophisticated, professional New York City bought our show. I sustained a terminal case of goose bumps. Imagine my pride!

Imagine my shock, then, when three months later we were canceled. WPIX had aired the show at 11 o'clock in the evening—directly against some of the highest-budgeted local newscasts in the country. We had bragged about attracting an audience that cares about issues, and then we found ourselves in the embarrassing position of trying to coax them away from the news. Hal Gold, the WPIX promotion man, tried all afternoon to find a New York newspaper reporter to interview me. When he failed, I felt more sorry for him than I did for me. On Channel 11 at 11 P.M. the *Donahue* show died—big. All of us wondered whether we'd get another shot at Mecca. Two years later, we did.

WNBC-TV Channel 4 in New York bought an edited half-hour version. The show is not a full half hour; after the commercials it is just 22 minutes. You can hardly say the Rosary in 22 minutes. Just about the time the discussion becomes airborne, I wave good-by. It was, however, the only offer we had, so of course we took it—nervously.

Despite the shortened show, we had more going for us than was true at WPIX. For one thing, we were on one of the most-watched and most prestigious television stations in the country—the flagship station of the mighty NBC Television Network. Our show got all the benefits: the peacock; the *Today* show adult-audience lead-in; the bonus of being sandwiched between two shows that at the time were doing well and enjoyed viewer respect, *Not for Women Only* with Barbara Walters and *Dinah's Place,* a half-hour network show which would later be unceremoniously canceled by someone who had an office at the most awe-inspiring address in broadcast history, 30 Rockefeller Plaza.

So there was Little Philly, right on the big stage between two big-league women—and whaddayaknow, he was doing okay. In about two months we realized two things: we were doing well, and WNBC was going to drive us crazy!

Every show we send to New York is screened by a member of the station's Standards and Practices Department. His job is to look for profanity, vulgarity, libel and any other material that might cause the station problems. It was during this time that I discovered "Lico-melli's Law," named after the man who has the job of determining whether tomorrow's *Donahue* show goes on the air in New York City. His name is Charles Licomelli, and the law named after him says, "If you appoint a censor, he will censor." Not to censor anything is to suggest that the station doesn't need a censor.

Curiously, of the more than seven hundred television stations in the United States, only a handful employ people to screen syndicated programs purchased by the station. In New York, where the stakes are high, the money is good and the pervasive paranoia has it that there's a shyster waiting for a chance to sue the Big Guys with the Big Bucks, censors are everywhere.

So into this cautious atmosphere comes *Donahue* with *The Sensuous Woman* (canceled because I carried the book around throughout the show and it "looked like a commercial"), Jacqueline Susann (canceled because she said, "I'd like to meet Philip Roth, but I wouldn't want to shake his hand")* and several other *Donahue* shows that never got on the air in "big, sophisticated" New York City.

By this time the show was five years old, we were airing in about forty cities and the only station canceling any of our shows was New York's WNBC-TV. We were angry and confused. From Dayton, Ohio, New York looked like the you-can't-shock-us town that we had read about. I mean, if New York can tolerate 42nd Street, it can certainly tolerate *Donahue.* Wrong!

---

* A reference to the famous descriptions of masturbation in Philip Roth's then best-selling novel *Portnoy's Complaint.*

In addition to the fear of harassing lawsuits, the network approach to daytime programming was also marked by paternalism and sexism. All the -ism's were against us. Somehow, WNBC felt a need to protect women from material it decided was too sexual or too visually explicit, like the film of hip-reduction surgery that showed the bare buttocks.

Material cleared for Johnny Carson at 11:30 P.M. was not cleared for me at 9:30 A.M. While it is true that more children might be exposed to my show than to the *Tonight* show, I nevertheless argued that our program was for adults; children are bored by our show; and further, if you make me decide all programming matters on the basis of possible child reaction, you reduce me to either *Captain Kangaroo* or slides and organ music. I begged. I argued. I raised my voice. I pouted. I said the shows they were canceling were airing in Atlanta and Buffalo and in every other *Donahue* city. Nothing worked. If NBC's Standards and Practices Department said no, the show did not air in New York. Regardless, the show remained number one, safely tucked away, at 9:30 A.M., between Barbara and Dinah.

For nine months we boasted about "airing on NBC in New York." It helped sell our show in Des Moines. Somehow, New York gives everybody else courage. The reasoning goes something like this: "If *Donahue* is carried by WNBC in New York, it can't be a bad show. Sold in Salt Lake."

New York should not have this kind of power, but it does, and we were exploiting it until, after nine months of broadcasts and a number one rating position, we were canceled and replaced by *It's Your Bet*, a game show. It remains the single most devastating blow sustained by the *Donahue* show. It retarded our growth by five years. "If you're canceled in New York, why should I buy you in Boise? No sale."

Our show was then six years old, and we no longer aired in New York. Despite our success in major markets like Philadelphia, Detroit, Atlanta, Cleveland and others, we did not have the respect of the biggies in our business because we did not air in New York or L.A. And I was frustrated. I was upset about being canceled and replaced by a game show. I was upset about the power of the networks and the arbitrary way they order affiliates and program suppliers around.

During a *Donahue* show featuring Bob Wussler, the president of the CBS Television Network, the dialogue went like this:

DONAHUE: How would *you* like to compete with [CBS]?
WUSSLER: You seem to be doing okay.

DONAHUE: But we're on very few CBS affiliate stations be-
            cause your network usurps all the air time.
WUSSLER: We just gave an hour back to the affiliates in the
            morning.
DONAHUE: Who said it was *yours* in the first place?

I was also upset because the networks were expanding soap operas
to one hour; and in Miami, our station, WCKT (an NBC affiliate), had
canceled *Donahue* because *Another World* was lengthened to an hour
and there was no room left on the daytime schedule.

I was disappointed because all the networks provided in the daytime was soaps and games.

I was disappointed because three giant companies control almost all
the air time in all the cities of America, and this power forces affiliates
to cower in fear of losing access to the big network nipple; and because the New York gatekeepers (the men who decide what and who
gets on American television) have the power to make or break careers
and TV programs.

I was concerned because somewhere there is a talented man or
woman who can produce a better program, execute a better talk show,
develop a new idea for exciting, unorthodox television; and he/she
will never get that opportunity because the networks have most of the
air time, and they are in the full-time business of not rocking the boat,
of protecting the great big number on the bottom line.

Finally, I was disappointed because we had had two times at bat in
New York and on both occasions struck out. I was convinced we
would never again get back into the ball game in Gotham.

And I was wrong again.

Donahue was nine years old when the show was purchased by
WOR-TV in New York City. Our third time at bat. We would never
be able to say we weren't given a chance. Once again I trundled to
New York for all the publicity hype—lunch with as many press as
would accept the invitation to come and meet the host of *Donahue*.
("Didn't he use to be on Channel Four, or was it Eleven?")

A small number of press people showed up, and I did my best to explain what we do. ("Just one guest per show? No band?")

I appeared on WOR-TV's noon information show, hosted by two
women, one of them married to the station's program director. She
opens the interview: "You bombed two other times in New York;
what makes you think you'll succeed now?" Welcome back to Charm
City!

After nine years on the air; scores of successes in most of America's major cities; an Emmy as best talk-show host; a move to Chicago, where we can more easily attract big-name guests, we were back in New York again to prove we were big-league material.

When I was told that WOR-TV had canceled us after six months, I wasn't shocked or even angry. I thought about how difficult it is to succeed with a syndicated product on an independent, non-network affiliate and, further, how difficult it is to explain that to anyone without sounding like "sour grapes." I thought about the woman who wanted to know, "What makes you think you'll make it this time?" And under my breath, I said, "Screw it," and went home and drank beer.

And so the *Donahue* show was about to celebrate its tenth anniversary without New York or Los Angeles. We were a very successful "Midwest" show. Good, but not great. We had become a candidate for a trivia quiz two decades hence, and I was a semistar—not Sinatra, not the weekend weatherman. I was spending a lot of time reviewing who I was and trying to find happiness in what was happening to me —even without New York and L.A.

We had produced a special program once on how some men get caught up in a numbers game and never really find happiness. In fact, the program cited evidence showing that a man with a numbers fixation usually died earlier of a heart attack. He was the Type A, who always counted the floors of a building or the trees in an orchard rather than enjoying their beauty. "What we need," said the doctor who developed the theory, "is more men who can enjoy watching minnows in a stream."

I will never forget the phrase "minnows in a stream" and the image of the Renaissance man that I wanted so much to be.

The doctor behind the theory was Meyer Friedman, M.D., and his book, *Type A Behavior & Your Heart,* catalogued the sins of the Type A, who has an impulsive need to accommodate every request for a favor ("He's too insecure to say no") and to constantly grow bigger. If he's a businessman with one store, he wants six, then twenty and so on. He is nervously on-the-go all the time. Sadly, his death usually comes before he has a chance to really enjoy his success. On vacations he constantly looks at his watch and seeks out *The Wall Street Journal.*

Type B, explained the doctor, is no less talented and is hardly lazy. He does, however, ration his time realistically. He is not insecure and often clears his mind for play or some leisure activity, thereby making him more capable of wise decisions when the time comes for them. Most corporation presidents are Bs—often because the As with whom they competed have died.

If ever I needed Dr. Friedman's theory, it was after being canceled in New York for the third time. I really worked at it. I reviewed the success of the show, told myself that literally millions of people every day were enjoying what we did and were learning from us. If the New York bureaucracy did not appreciate what we did or couldn't understand it, that was New York's loss, not mine. I could live without New York—I already had for forty years. Screw New York! And that, as my Notre Dame math teacher would say after concluding a long equation on the blackboard, "is the way it must always be."

Except for one man.

Just when I had reluctantly concluded that New York would never be mine and that glory for me rested somewhere between both coasts but not on them, just when I had started to get comfortable with my Type B behavior and applaud myself for not being the blindly ambitious television type that pursues the top at all costs, just when I had begun to adapt to the realization that I would never be a biggie—just when I began to think about minnows in a stream—one man came along and gave me the chance I'd never thought would ever come my way again, the chance to be a hit in New York and become the *number one* syndicated-talk-show host in the nation.

The man was Stanley Siegel.

I first met Stanley in Don Dahlman's office in Dayton. Don was the general manager of the station from which the show aired for its first six years. He hired me, stood up to the hate mail when gays and atheists appeared on the show, never once said, "Why in hell did you do that?" went out and single-handedly sold the program in syndication, and served as emotional anchor for me during my marriage breakup. He and his wife, Babs, are the two finest people I have met in broadcasting, and he is the man who is most responsible for a decade of *Donahue* that brought us so much challenge and excitement.

When I walked into Don's office, he introduced me to a pleasant-looking man about my age. Stanley said he had worked in Green Bay, Wisconsin, and said, among other things, that he had once driven a Volkswagen into a lake to see if it would float—as claimed by an ad campaign. He also had submerged himself in a tub of Jell-O. It was clear that Stanley was good at getting attention—and liked to talk about his bizarre stunts. He was his own best cheerleader. At the time, he was looking for work and thought maybe Don Dahlman could help him.

Several years later, Stanley would tell *New York* magazine that while employed in Nashville, he had watched me tape a program with Burt Reynolds at WSM and been convinced that he could do a better interview. The article came out at the same time that WNBC announced it had purchased the *Donahue* show for airing weekdays at 9—right smack against you-know-who.

By the time the decision was made to send *Donahue* after Siegel, Stanley was enjoying the biggest victory of his career. Following a long line of famous and not-so-famous hosts on *A.M. New York* on WABC-TV, Stanley had become the first host to succeed in the ratings. His most-talked-about air feature was a weekly confrontation with a real live psychiatrist. Viewers were treated to a grimly open discussion of Stanley's personal feelings and latest crises. In most sessions he shared right on the air details of his most personal problems. It was better than a tub of Jell-O and a floating Volkswagen combined, and it sure got the public's attention.

It also succeeded in getting lots of media interest. Stanley, a local personality in New York, had already enjoyed a full-page article in *Newsweek* (news is what New York says is news) and a lengthy positive column in *New York* magazine, not to mention several newspaper references to this latter-day Jack Paar—who was even more personal on the air and often more outrageous.

So there was Stanley, scoring big in the Big Time. He was leading *Concentration* on NBC by two to one when my phone rang. My mission—and I immediately chose to accept it—was to knock off Stanley and get WNBC-TV back into the number one position following the handsome lead-in of the *Today* show. I was up to bat again in the biggest park of 'em all—for the fourth time. And I knew in my soul that as far as *Donahue* and New York were concerned, this was definitely the last of the ninth. I was convinced that I would never again know this kind of pressure.

Already the New York press was speculating about what *Cue* magazine called "Star Wars in the Morning"—with squared-off pictures of me and Stanley. After ten years on the air and almost three thousand shows, it all came down to the battle of the hang-ups. And worse, Stanley was making a lot of noise by talking about his neuroses while I was handicapped by the conventional policy of discussing problems in a general way with guest psychiatrists. I had nightmares of a bland *Donahue* show featuring a "talking head" on sexual dysfunction while

Stanley was over there on Channel 7 showing slides of his last intimate encounter.

Once again I was angry with the networks and their power. Why had WNBC waited so long to buy our show? Why had WABC had to hire Stanley and start to score before WNBC saw the futility of sending *Concentration* after him? Why had WNBC canceled our show five years before? Why does a success in New York matter so much? Where are you, Dr. Friedman?

We were about one month to the premiere date of our show on WNBC-TV in New York when Stanley Siegel upped the ante in the morning crap game tenfold. Like most things Stanley did, it was an unplanned, ad-libbed event that caused real pain to a person who matters to me—very much.

Marlo was promoting a movie, and her New York schedule called for her to appear on "something called *The Stanley Siegel Show*." (Stanley's success gave him the power to demand a change from the old *A.M. New York* title.)

During his introduction, Stanley, without notes or warning, said, "Marlo is of the Lebanese persuasion. Part of their religion is to hate the Jews."

Marlo's response was more than disbelief—it was shock and then anger. The viewers saw her marching off the set behind Stanley as he rambled on in his disconnected monologue. The whole crew is watching the off-camera drama, and everyone is confused.

Marlo is between a rock and a hard place. If she exits, she leaves his defamation of the Lebanese people unchallenged; if she stays, she not only boosts the ratings of the show, but also has to spend an hour with a man who may "go off" again at any time. His humor makes the Polish joke look like a Hallmark card.

Marlo stays.

Stanley begins the interview as though nothing had happened. Marlo interrupts him. "Wait a minute!" she says. "How can you, in this time of unrest and human suffering in the Middle East, make such an irresponsible and untrue remark?"

Stanley tells Marlo she has no sense of humor. He says he was just kidding, and Marlo says his comment was the most unfunny line she has ever heard and stiffly resists his attempts to hug her and make her agree that all is forgiven.

Stanley is relentless. "My folks live near your folks in Beverly Hills," he says.

He says again that he was just kidding, and she says again that it wasn't funny; and when it was over, I had the feeling that Stanley had succeeded, through the victimization of Marlo Thomas, in providing New York viewers with another memorable television experience. Sort of like watching an auto accident.

Meanwhile, over on WNBC-TV, contestants were trying to match the squares of a puzzle on *Concentration*. And very few viewers were watching.

It is *High Noon* in my career, and I am not at all sure that I am Gary Cooper. Nevertheless, I had to, as they say on Monday-night football, "go for it." First there were another press luncheon at "21," a round of the talk shows in New York, including the Bill Boggs show and others. The final event of a whirlwind promotion trip to New York City was a visit to—believe it or not—*The Stanley Siegel Show!* Stanley, in the tradition of Jell-O and Volkswagens, had invited *me* to appear on *his* show!

First, the luncheon. It was hosted by Bob Howard, the general manager of WNBC-TV. We had a private room upstairs at "21," and there was a very large turnout of reporters: Val Adams, New York *Daily News;* Dan Lewis, Bergen *Record;* Katie Kelley, *New York Post;* Marvin Kitman, *Newsday;* John Dempsey, *Variety;* Estelle Wallach, *Essence* magazine; Bruce Blackwell, Westchester-Rockland Papers. I thought of Hal Gold at WPIX. Oh, that network power! I am seated at one of the round tables with Howard, WNBC station manager Ann Berk, program director Dave Chase.

I was trying not to sound like a vacuum-cleaner salesman while at the same time offering information that might or might not find its way into print. I was mouthing statements about our show which I have offered to countless television critics at scores of newspapers around the country.

If there was a quiver in my voice, it was because I knew that this was It—my last shot at New York. I reviewed the bidding to myself: If we make it here, it means a certain chance at L.A.; and success in New York and L.A. is the whole ball game. If we make it in those cities, all we have to do is answer the phone and take orders from everywhere else in the country.

"There are five people who produce the program," I say, "three women and two men. I'm one of the men. We argue, we read a lot of magazines, steal ideas from other shows [the reporters' faces brighten at the candor] and get a lot of program suggestions from viewers.

"While we are very pleased that Bob Hope and Johnny Carson and a host of other biggies have done our show, the fact remains that our program survives on issues. We discuss more issues, more often, more thoroughly than any other show in the business.

"We also involve the audience in our act more than any other show on the air, period. Without the audience, there's no *Donahue* show."

Some of the reporters were taking notes; most were not. The luncheon was moving along as planned, and I thought I was succeeding in not looking too desperate or too solicitous. Suddenly it happened. What I feared the most happened. The name of Stanley Siegel came up. For the better part of half an hour, the New York television critics offered their own assessments of Stanley Siegel. I sustained a severe anxiety attack. I needed Stanley's shrink. Any shrink.

On Friday morning, October 21, 1977, a little over three weeks after *Donahue* premiered on Channel 4, *The Stanley Siegel Show* featured Phil Donahue and a female impersonator on Channel 7. I showed up at the 67th Street studio at 8:30 A.M., a full half hour before air. I was in the makeup chair when Stanley walked in. I knew the moment I saw him he was nervous. I wondered why he was doing this. I concluded he was more interested in nurturing his image as a man filled with uncanny surprises than he was in providing any promotion for me or my show.

As for me, I figured I couldn't lose. I was in effect plugging into Stanley's audience and, if nothing else, letting them know that I was on the other station and—without saying so out loud—hoping they would be encouraged to give me a try. I was also very keyed up for Stanley; and, although quite nervous myself, I honestly became convinced that I was more in charge of the situation than he was. I decided to take the offensive.

During the live tease in the station break preceding Stanley's show, the three of us—me, Stanley and the female impersonator—stood—like the McGuire sisters—facing the camera while Stanley ad-libbed the guests on his upcoming show. In the middle of his comments and without warning, I suddenly placed my arm around Stanley's shoulder and interrupted, "We eat well, get plenty of sleep and exercise, take Geritol every day—and I love him."

It worked. It was funny. The crew laughed. Score one for Little Philly at the O.K. Corral.

Stanley opened his show and said something about there being "only one of us alive" when the show concluded. He was gamely trying to be funny, but his nervousness showed—I thought, more than mine. And then he began the interview.

"Are you nervous?" he asked. Stanley said he thought I looked nervous. He said he knew I was Catholic and he said he was Jewish, but regardless, he thought we had much in common.

I offered that Catholics and Jews have similar hang-ups—including sexism, which I thought was very much a part of both traditions.

"How's that?" he asked.

I said that there's a Jewish prayer which in effect has men thanking God they are not women. I also said very few Jewish women are basmitzvahed.

Stanley wasn't sure that was true, but a cameraman was vigorously nodding affirmatively at me and I began to feel a little better. A frog kept sticking in my throat, and I couldn't seem to dislodge it. I kept trying to clear it—midway through all my answers. My body temperature was up, and I felt traces of perspiration on my forehead.

Once again, Stanley wanted to know if I was nervous. His questions about nervousness were making me nervous.

Suddenly Stanley reached down next to his chair and—like a magician—displayed a huge cardboard rectangle on which were printed a series of numbers. While trying to analyze the visual aid and catch up with Stanley's comments, I realized he had a huge photostat of a page from a Nielsen rating book.

"Here are some ratings I want the audience to see," Stanley said proudly. Sure enough, there were Channels 7, 4, 2, 5 and all the other numbers to which New Yorkers automatically flip for the widest choice of television programming anywhere in the world.

My eyes squinted at the numbers under the hot studio lights, and Stanley's hand went immediately to the Channel 7 column and the number displayed next to the 9-o'clock time period. A 3.2. Next to Channel 4, a 2.1. While the cameraman jockeyed into position for a close shot, Stanley was telling viewers up and down the East Coast of America that he was definitely beating Phil Donahue in the ratings race. To myself I was saying, You son of a bitch!

Just as suddenly a voice from behind the camera said—with some urgency—"That's August!" It was Stanley's own producer, himself taken aback by a maneuver his own man had apparently not discussed with him. The weight was off my shoulders, and I made another big move.

"Stanley, you're showing August figures and I wasn't even on the air then. C'mon, Stanley!"

Up to now Stanley had been just plain nervous; now he was shook.

I could see moisture on his forehead, and I continued the advance—throat-frog and all.

Cautious about sounding too patronizing, I lectured Stanley on "not putting all your eggs in a ratings basket." Could Stanley forget about ratings for a whole week? No, he couldn't. Well, then, said the visiting guru, Stanley is not getting the most out of life. "Ratings can be a very unreliable life prop," I pontificated. "A man ought to enjoy watching minnows in a stream."

Stanley was on the ropes, and for the first time that morning I felt totally confident. The interview continued.

"How's Marlo?" Stanley asked.

"Fine."

"She was on my show, y'know."

"Yeah, I know." I was beginning to feel like Gary Cooper. I was ready.

Stanley said he couldn't understand why Marlo had been so upset—he had just been kidding. And besides, his folks lived near her folks in Beverly Hills. "All I said was that the Arabs dislike the Jews."

I leaned forward in my chair. "You didn't say dislike; you said *hate*. It was the most untalented thing you ever said in your life. In an age of hijackings and shootings and terrorism, this is not a humorous subject."

The frog in my throat was gone.

When it ended, Stanley was still on his feet but wobbly. I knew I had scored. I had successfully introduced myself to Stanley's audience, many of whom were loyal Siegel watchers who wanted this shy, insecure, vulnerable man-child to win. I had made it clear that while Stanley was on Channel 7 at 9 A.M. weekdays, Donahue was on Channel 4 at the same time. It was like a free commercial on the competing station.

On the following Wednesday, Stanley lay down on his couch—on the air—and told his shrink with painful candor that "Phil Donahue destroyed me; why did I put him on? I hated myself all day."

Meanwhile over at WNBC-TV, Charlie Licomelli (still on the job) was reviewing all the *Donahue* programs before air and approving almost all of them. The hassles that we experienced earlier under "Licomelli's Law" were now almost nonexistent. Stanley had created an entirely new atmosphere for morning television in New York City. Now, almost anything goes.

Gradually our ratings improved. The New York press was still giving combat reports on the morning "Star Wars." WCBS-TV was now in the battle with the new syndicated *Jim Nabors Show*. The numbers watchers and the graph plotters were sending out for coffee. The press was offering almost weekly reports. Donahue and Siegel neck and neck. Nabors trailing.

Slowly our show began to pull away. We enjoyed a tremendous advantage with the dominant *Today* show lead-in—which, despite *Good Morning America* successes in some cities, continued to place number one in the early-morning competition in New York. Dinah and Barbara were gone from the morning NBC New York lineup, and there was Mr. Dayton, Ohio, hanging on to the lead spot for a whole hour.

Shortly thereafter, WCBS canceled the Nabors show. Casualty count: one dead, one wounded. After six months on the air in New York, *Donahue* was attracting almost as many adult viewers as WABC and WCBS *combined*. I couldn't have been more pleased. Or more surprised.

Suddenly my phone was ringing. *Newsweek, McCall's, Cosmopolitan, Good Housekeeping,* American Airlines' in-flight magazine and *Oui* all wanted to do stories on "the *new* talk-show host from Chicago." *TV Guide* wanted to do a cover; so did *People*. Get it? A cover! (News is what New York says is news.)

And the coup de grâce: Joe Bartelme, an NBC vice-president, called to ask if I'd be interested in hosting the *Today* show. I said, "What young American boy wouldn't be?" And he came to Chicago and we talked.

Then I went to New York for dinner with Paul Friedman, executive producer of *Today*. I was not sure I wanted the job. I cautiously avoided any clichés at dinner because I wanted to impress him. In my heart I knew that after all the shlepping, all the cancellations, all the frustrations with the power brokers, I was, at age 42, after nine years of news, five years of *Conversation Piece* and ten years of *Donahue*, finally—as New York would say—"hot."

Back in Cincinnati, my own employers were anxiously reading about their star and trying to talk me into a new contract. I was saying to myself that going to New York, buying the big expensive apartment, plugging all the boys into school and then a year later having some unknown vice-president cancel me while he's shaving was not what I had worked my butt off for all these years. I knew I couldn't abandon what I had spent ten years trying to build—especially when it appeared we had finally acquired the power that was so elusive without New York City.

Besides, while there's very little security in this business, I had more than most on-camera folks. For example, if the show is canceled in Peoria, I'm still alive in Philadelphia and so on. Unlike Stanley or any of the network faces, I did not have all my eggs in one ratings vice-president's basket. I was also free of the whims of insecure network decision makers who can make a lot of unnecessary waves. One gate-keeper couldn't kill me.

I signed a new six-year contract with Multimedia. KTLA in Los Angeles bought our show, and suddenly we were in 178 markets, more than any other syndicated talk show on the air. I was, at last, and beyond my wildest fantasy, number one in my game.

We were on the air for six weeks in L.A. and it became apparent that we were not going to burn the town down. On independent Channel 5 the *Donahue* show was pulling an unspectacular 1.6 rating, and I was thinking, Please God, not again.

In *Variety* I read that Stanley Siegel had failed to come to terms with WABC-TV and had been separated from the station. And I went home and drank beer.

Shortly thereafter, it was announced that WCBS-TV in New York City had hired Stanley to host a half-hour talk show. The nationally circulated *New Times* magazine published a lengthy article about Stanley (News is what New York . . .) in which he is quoted as saying, "They say Phil beat me. Actually old people watch Donahue. The young women, 18 to 49, watch me."

Again I reviewed my life, my values, my priorities and my feelings. If I had scored such a clean victory, why did I feel so ambivalent? Why am I so competitive? I thought about all those fights I had as a kid. Is the reward worth the rancor? Why the lies, the put-downs? Perhaps Stanley and Phil should both be watching "minnows in a stream."

Part of my anxiety stemmed from my own reluctant admission that despite my lofty speeches about the value of Type B behavior, I was without a doubt a Type A and making very little progress toward changing. Like that of the man who counts floors in a building and trees in an orchard, my emotional well-being remained unbecomingly attached to a number. The number was 178, the total cities that carried *Donahue*.

I could hear Stanley telling the reporter that "old people watch Donahue" and under my breath I heard myself saying, "Screw Stanley Siegel." And I went home and drank beer.

Hype

HENRY FONDA (on the Academy Awards): "Well, I just don't think it's possible to say [who is best actor]. Woody Allen did his very best, Laurence Olivier did his very best. . . . I just say you can't compare them."

DONAHUE: "What would you do, get rid of the Academy Awards?"

FONDA: "I am told not to talk about that because it's against the industry. I do recognize that it's the big public relations moment for the industry."

This exchange on a recent *Donahue* program reflects the growing influence of promotion upon American media. The Academy Awards, originally conceived to honor achievement, have become a vehicle for selling tickets.

In fact, to the movie industry, the promotional value of the Academy Awards has become so important that nervous studio moguls have muzzled superstars who would criticize them.

The play's not the thing: the hype is.

Promotion has actually become its own billion-dollar industry, and its influence is being felt in not-so-subtle ways on television and in the print media.

The union of America's expanding, well-financed promotion industry and the media is one of the more ominous developments of the communications era. The business of hype and the business of journalism shouldn't be married. In fact, they make no effort to hide their disdain for each other in public. Journalists complain that the P.R. people try to manipulate the news; P.R. people accuse the media of bias and "sensationalism" which unfairly damage the image of the big businessmen they are paid to protect.

Imagine their surprise, then, when the hype people and the journalism "virgins" suddenly found themselves in the same bed.

America's talk-variety-information shows, including *Today, Tonight, Tomorrow, The Merv Griffin Show,* the *Mike Douglas Show, Dinah, Good Morning America, Donahue* and scores of local programs have become not a forum for sharing ideas, but a platform for pitchmen. A "talking head" on any of these shows is usually a person who is trying to sell a book, an album or a movie ticket.

During 1978, *Donahue* presented a total of 236 hour-long programs, 122 of which had featured guests who were trying to sell something. Fifty-six per cent! The greedy hand of hype has extended so totally into television that today's talk-show viewers are dismayed to discover that what they're watching between "all those commercials" . . . is another commercial.

This is not to say that authors and movie stars have no business on talk shows: rather, that the system of "touring" them for sales promotion has become so high-powered that many talk-show producers have surrendered their programs to the publicity agents. All TV producers need do is wait for the phone to ring. And it surely will. Calling will be the representatives of famous and not-so-famous people who are under orders to get out and sell. In today's talk-show industry, the "parts supplier" is wagging the "factory."

We can only speculate about how many worthy folks with exciting new ideas are never exposed to television audiences because a publisher has succeeded in "booking" the authors of *How to Be Your Own Best Friend* ("It's now out in paperback!") and in the words of the grateful and relieved talk-show producer, "We're all set for Tuesday." The pressure from publishers to feature authors is so intense that the decision about who gets on television is often made not by the people who work for *Today,* but by Doubleday.

Television is not the exclusive target of promoters. The friendly folks at the print media are also going to lunch with the hype people. Is *Superman* really worthy of a *Newsweek* cover? Anyone who paid $3 to see the movie must have wondered if P. T. Barnum hadn't underestimated the population of suckers. Nevertheless, the decision is made to feature *Superman* on the cover, and the loyal *Newsweek* staffers (mortgage holders all) are obliged to write the story. And how much hard-hitting, irreverent journalism can we expect from the final product? Consider this paragraph from *Newsweek*'s cover story:

> Although "Superman" has flaws of pace, structure, and concept, Donner's [Richard, the director] shaping of the film amounts in its way to a major feat of filmmaking.

Which is like a television reviewer saying:

> Although Donahue's guest gave long, rambling answers, the audience appeared listless and the host himself was unprepared, the program was one of the major achievements of the television talk show in America.

Add to this the gala Washington premiere of *Superman*, attended by President Jimmy Carter and his daughter, Amy, and you have some idea of the power of twentieth-century promotion. And if *Newsweek* will bend its copy so as not to condemn the subject of its own cover story, how much aggressive interviewing can we expect from nervous and grateful talk-show hosts who succeed in "getting Sophia Loren first"? Will Donahue say the autobiography of the Italian actress is not that revealing? (I didn't.)

In short, America may not be reading an objective cover story, or watching a candid interview on television. What may be happening right before our eyes is a not so thinly disguised sales pitch.

The ever-present effort to use these public vehicles for promotion has reduced the space and time for originally developed ideas and diminished the energy of journalists and talk-show producers to innovate and search out that "woman-fights-city-hall" feature which might be a lot more enlightening than a *Superman* story and a lot more entertaining than the breathless actress who gushes to the host about "the incredible script, incredible cast and incredible director. I'm incredibly excited."

Another unbecoming feature of the relationship between marketing and media that bears watching is the increasing use of charity to sell goods and services. McDonald's has used television to announce a charity donation for every Big Mac sold, and Jerry Lewis stands in front of 7-Eleven urgently exhorting America to shop there—and to leave the change for "my kids."

The enthusiasm that moves giant companies to push and shove in order to get a hold on the charity coattail is no more evident than on the *Jerry Lewis Telethon* tote board. The display, which automatically tallies the weekend receipts, is crowned by a huge clock surrounded by a logo informing viewers all over America that Helbros is the "Official Timekeeper" of the *Jerry Lewis Telethon.* What's a telethon without an "official" timekeeper, and how generous of Helbros to provide this indispensable service for free!

On one occasion I flew to Sacramento to take part in a fund-raiser for the Sacramento Symphony Orchestra. When I arrived, Ronald McDonald and several photographers met me at the airport. Ronald McDonald also met me at my hotel. Flashbulbs exploded and news cameras whirred as he shook my hand. (Ronald has also helped me answer phones on several local telethons.)

Antique cars carried the celebrities and the "Friends of Symphony" to a twenties style fashion show featuring merchandise available at a local Sacramento department store—artfully noted in the program— and then the whole V.I.P. entourage sputtered away in vintage vehicles to see the Sacramento premiere of *The Great Gatsby.* We all filed past a smiling theater owner as photographers blazed away.

The Sacramento Symphony was the "do-good" feature of the gala evening, and everybody—including me—was in on the sell. McDonald was selling French-fries, the department store was selling apparel, the movie guy was selling what he hoped would be a hot picture—and Donahue was selling himself to a Northern California city so the broadcasting industry wouldn't type him as "Midwest."

Who was using whom?

The charity telethon is a study in disorganization and self-congratulation.

On the telethon phone (I have answered scores of them), a man with bad grammar and slurred speech is asking me if I'll announce that all the people at the Y'All Come Back Lounge want to challenge all the other taverns in the western part of the city to contribute to "your telethon there. . . . We collected twenty-eight dollars and we wanna challenge the other bars. . . ." He also wants to know if I'll "mention the tavern on TV."

In another part of the television studio a local cowboy band is playing "Help Me Make It Through the Night" at half speed while the host,* tie grandly loosened, drinks coffee out of a paper cup and moves about the room in a visual demonstration of perseverance, endurance, caring and hard work. In the lobby, the president of a local C.B. club, wearing a bright red Eisenhower-style jacket that says BREAKER BREAKER, is trying to get into the studio so he can "challenge all the C.B.-ers in the city" to donate money to the telethon.

It is a zoo.

It is also unfair and inefficient, and divisive.

Nowhere are America's screwed-up priorities more evident than here. Meeting the needs of crippled children ought to be a part of citizenship and not dependent on the goodwill of a popular entertainer or the benevolence of a television-station operator, who may or may not hand over his facilities for one entire weekend. Money for research into catastrophic diseases ought to be provided out of the taxes that Americans pay. We don't have telethons or bike-a-thons or walk-a-thons for highways or airports; why must we resort to this loosely organized and often unsuccessful Roman circus to raise funds for our children?

The all-time vulgarity of misguided charity do-good-ism occurred in Peoria, Illinois, in early 1979—a "drink-a-thon" held to benefit the Peoria Association for Retarded Citizens. The report said, "About 20 people drank in the event which netted an estimated 15-hundred dollars for the association." Volunteers agreed to drink in every bar on Peoria's Adams Street from 10 A.M. to 6:30 P.M. One drinker said, "The hardest part was having only one drink in each bar." The story ran complete with a photo of a volunteer, unconsciously drunk along the roadway, and the lead, "The amount raised wasn't staggering . . ." What is not so funny is that the press plays into this kind of feature story without the slightest notice of how this absurdity blinds us to the importance of funding worthy projects responsibly.

The celebrity-telethon package comes complete with a producer who will direct the time and the amount of increase on the tote board, withholding fund totals until the maximum excitement is generated at just the right moment. He will also use audio tapes of phones ringing, creating the illusion of much viewer interest and excitement (like a laugh track). The host will say, "The phones are starting to ring. Reach into your pocket . . ."

The phones at telethons are staffed by chiefs of police, banking vice-presidents and judges, all busily talking on the phone behind

---

* Hosts on local telethons are sometimes paid for their participation. I have been offered (and refused) $5,000 to host a local telethon for a children's hospital.

large signs which identify not only the phone answerer but his company or position as well. Only occasionally will the volunteer glance up to see if he's on camera.

America's charity business places U.S. media moguls in the no-win position of having to decide who gets the use of their airwaves for telethons or money appeals of any kind. If the television general manager chooses to carry the *Jerry Lewis Telethon,* does this mean he can, without feelings of guilt, turn down the local Variety Club for the children's hospital? How many telethons is a television station obliged to carry in a year? How is the choice to be made? If television stations donate their facilities for fund-raising efforts, why doesn't the telephone company donate its phones for pledge taking? Who makes these vital decisions that affect research into disease, hospitals, the sick? Should television executives and movie stars decide who gets our money? I don't think so.

The system is unfair because it relies on the goodwill of famous and powerful people for success. Whether or not your "favorite charity" (a curious choice of words) has fund-raising capability depends on whether you can encourage a celebrity to speak for it. The inequality of the system is also apparent in the promotional benefits of the "Poster Child." Spina bifida children will receive more research money than cystic fibrosis kids—because the latter have no visible handicap. C.F. victims may not live past 26 years of age, but you'd never know it to look at the poster.

The system is also inefficient, because the event by which the charity raises funds is often more cumbersome and expensive than the small net proceeds of the evening justify. On one such occasion I sat in one of Chicago's largest hotel ballrooms as hundreds of Chicago's finest and richest couples danced to the music of Peter Duchin and then sat back under the smoke of expensive cigars to sip champagne and watch Noriko present her latest fashion collection. An elegant evening indeed. And an expensive one.

I have no doubt that those in attendance were well motivated and wanted very much to ensure the continued vitality of the beneficiary—an institution for the retarded. My problem with this kind of "gala" is that by the time you pay for the ballroom, the caterer, the bartenders, the union models and the society orchestra, the amount left over for the charity is not all that impressive.

Moreover, when the doctor finally steps on the stage to receive the check from the ball chairperson, the amount is usually within reach of any one of a number of fat cats looking on from behind their long cigars. An elephant has given birth to a mouse.

Inefficiency is ensured in the voluntary charity game because events which attach themselves to a do-good fund-raising effort are often not asked to account for their proceeds publicly. Is a public audit on all these events in order? More simply: may we see the check, please?

Finally, the system of volunteerism is also divisive. It pits one charity against the others for the charity dollar, which is suffering from the double whammy of inflation and diminished philanthropic zeal on the part of those beleaguered American citizens who wonder more and more why they have to bear the cost of an Israeli–Egyptian peace settlement and the local Girl Scout troop as well.

Into this challenge step America's advertising agencies, which (often for a fee) will provide some of the most creative campaigns in history—all designed to squeeze another dollar out of the wallet of a reluctant and guilt-ridden giver. Thus, the "Neediest Children's Fund" campaign is intended to suggest that here, ladies and gentlemen, are not the needy kids, but the *neediest*. Here is where your hard-earned charity dollar should go. (Worry about the just plain *needy* kids later?)

We have allowed the charity business to become as competitive as any marketing fight between Colgate and Procter and Gamble.

No wonder the Heart Fund has little good to say about the United Appeal, which used to suggest deceptively that your one gift covered everything. Today, while your "one gift works many wonders," those "wonders" do not express themselves at the Leukemia Society, or the Cancer Society, or Easter Seals, or countless other charities not a part of "the United Way." There is also evidence that "Mother Charity" is being used to nurse personal careers.

More than one radio program director has written a memo encouraging his disc jockeys, all of whom are in constant rating battles for their lives, to get involved in telethons, bike-a-thons, walk-a-thons (I once interviewed a D.J. who rocked in a rocker for fourteen hours to raise money for Easter Seals. A rock-a-thon?) or any other charity-thon that will draw crowds of people and TV cameras in search of a feature story for the 6-o'clock news.

Businessmen have also found the charity handle.

The July 1979 issue of *Fortune* magazine features a cover story titled "Repackaging the Executive," which details the work done by image-building companies in the highly paid business of "shaping" business executives for promotion. The article reported, without blanching, "Consultants channel their clients into public-service activities that will win kudos . . . and press coverage. They'll even ghostwrite the acceptance speech." Sort of "The Selling of the [Business] Vice-President."

My views of the charity game come from countless experiences wherein I was the celebrity at the fund-raising ball, banquet, softball game, shoeshine-in, tennis tournament, pro–am golf tournament or telethon. I have wiped saliva off the mouths of spastics straining against the straps of their wheelchairs to greet me, and I have met their parents, who refuse to surrender and who continue to give their love—without fanfare, or plaques, or dinners, or any of the other ways we honor athletes and "stars" and other high-visibility people who already get more attention than is good for them.

I have talked with the father of a spina bifida child, and he looked as though he wasn't sure what had hit him. I have counted my blessings, and I have been encouraged to worry about the *important* things. I have been reminded that all of us—in parenthood—are one chromosome away from a brain-damaged child or an offspring with a disfigured body.

The awareness makes the "business" of speaking to the needs of these children and their parents more urgent. I believe that the "business" is in desperate need of critical examination. What we have now is *not* better than nothing. What we have is a badly constructed system that is at the same time struggling to keep up with growing needs and lulling Americans into thinking it is doing a good job—and that contributions and "celebrity appearances" can solve the problems of human misery.

As long as we continue to congratulate ourselves for working on the "gala" charity dinner, or the telethon, or the celebrity auction, as long as we applaud people who sit in rockers in furniture-store windows or sleep on flagpoles for charity, as long as we allow popular entertainers to determine the recipient of our philanthropy, we delay the time when we finally face up to the painful fact that this country's priorities are wrong. The health of our children—*all* of our children—should come first. Sick children ought to receive as large a piece of our public-money pie as municipal stadia, superhighways and swing-wing bombers.

Perhaps our tax money should go toward the solving of children's health problems, and the Pentagon should be allowed to have a telethon for war!

In far too many instances, charity has become something for rich people to do, with focus on the stars, not on the charity itself—or its purpose. Show business should be out of *this* business, and parents who have to deal with the emotional blow of caring for a special child should know that the money is there for research and special institutional care, not because an entertainer consented to speak for them, but because this country has reordered its priorities so that public money is allocated *first* for the sick child, and *second* for the businessman who wants to fly in a faster airplane that needs a longer runway.

America should not tolerate companies that create merchandising campaigns in conjunction with charities. No box tops for the retarded, no coupons, no summer camp for kids based on used-car sales. Or any sales.

We should not use crippled children to sell hamburgers. Ever.

18

The Faint-hearted Feminist

ONCE, DURING a week of *Donahue* shows from Atlanta, I was driving to our station, WAGA-TV. As I proceeded down Briarcliff Road I glanced in the rearview mirror and saw Darlene Hayes driving behind me. To her right in the front seat sat our guest for that day. His head was not totally visible above the dashboard, which in my mirror appeared to cut across the bottom of his chin. The man's ever-devoted wife sat in the back seat. Because there were only three along for the ride, she sat alone. Darlene told me later that she took part in no conversation en route to the television station that morning. She knew her place and had long since made peace with it. She was Josephine Hoffa, wife of the late president of the International Brotherhood of Teamsters, the largest and most powerful union in the history of the American labor movement.*

Recently, during a trip to a smaller California city, the general manager of the station there agreed to chauffeur Marlo and me to the airport. I cannot explain why this is important to me, and I am not altogether comfortable with the fact that it is. It all happened so fast.

---

* Later, after the program, Jimmy Hoffa told a press conference that when he first came to Georgia in the thirties they tried to "get Hoffa" and they'd been trying to "get Hoffa" ever since. As if awed by his own persona, he continued to use the third person when speaking of himself. His visit to my program coincided with his campaign for prison reform following his release from a federal penitentiary, a move engineered by the Oval Office. Two years later, outside the Red Fox restaurant in suburban Detroit, someone finally succeeded in the long conspiracy to "get Hoffa." I will always wonder whether Jimmy Hoffa's last ride was in the back seat or the front seat.

The three of us were en route to the airport when I suddenly realized that I was in the back seat. Alone. There was Marlo in an animated conversation with the driver, and there I was—America's number one syndicated-talk-show host—in the back seat, for Chrissake! Like I was Josephine Hoffa. I was embarrassed to say, even to Marlo, that it caused me suffering.

Now that I have had time to analyze my feelings, I am certain that they are totally neurotic, sexist, silly and a big waste of time. I have even set up mental exercises to determine which situation bothers me the most. For example, I am not troubled if Marlo is in the back seat and I am in the front seat. I am only slightly troubled if Marlo is in the front seat and I am in the back along with other people. Nevertheless, I am clear about wanting to be in the same seat with Marlo in all vehicles. I am determined—and this is the embarrassing part—to be on constant guard against sharing a ride with Marlo and occupying the back seat alone!

This is just one of countless little tests that our changing culture has placed before Little Philly in his middle years to keep him off guard and sometimes uptight. It is another reminder that proclaiming feminism and practicing it usually mark the difference between the truly committed and the Big Mouth.

My relationship with Marlo is the first I have ever had in which the woman has had so much time and energy and enthusiasm for people other than me. She receives more phone calls in a week than all the other people I have ever escorted to a dance floor put together. She has gotten more laughs and drawn the attention of more men and women than anybody I ever met at the St. Christopher Canteen. ("She had a dark and a rovin' eye, and her hair hung down in ring-a-lets . . .")

Marlo is a constant reminder of how much I have changed and how much I have remained the same. One Saturday afternoon in Winnetka, while I was en route to the drugstore, the network news on the car radio announced that "Forty thousand people, led by actress Marlo Thomas, marched in Washington today in the biggest demonstration yet in favor of the Equal Rights Amendment." Later that evening I would pout because she didn't call.

I have learned only slowly about the "ism" of feminism—not by knowing the lines ("kids get too much mother and not enough father") but by knowing feminists themselves. I have observed—close up —the care and love they have for each other, for battered wives and for women in the office who are not only not promoted but sexually harassed as well. And I have seen their anger at rape jokes, insensitive doctors and unnecessary hysterectomies, as well as unpaid child support, pill side effects and teen-age pregnancies. And I have begun to understand why feminists are occasionally accused of being humorless.

I have come to understand that feminists do not long for an either/or world. It is not a matter of strong or weak, or hard or soft, or front seat or back seat. It is a matter of sharing opportunities like child rearing and breadwinning, of sharing life. I have learned that sometimes feminists are weak and insecure and will ask for help. And sometimes they will *give* it.

I have also learned that most feminists like sex, good music, dancing, good wine and male-chauvinist pigs who are trying. They can also sense from afar M.C.P.s who are not trying.

But the learning has not been easy. Egalitarian attitudes and respect for women's ability were not born and nurtured in a childhood grammar-school experience that saw scores of boys serve Mass and only one girl a year granted the honor of crowning the statue of the Blessed Mother during May ceremonies. Moreover, it was the *boys* who held the flags after school that said STOP, and it was the boys who had uniforms and teams and stronger bicycles. The girls had the brains, but the boys had the power.

Imagine how threatening it is to a former altar boy finding himself, thirty years later, in the company of women who are not only smart but eager for power as well. Sometimes I become angry at their stridency and their arrogant you've-got-a-long-way-to-go-baby attitude. I raise my voice and say, "We men did not *invent* this culture. We are entitled to some understanding. Of course there are abuses, but because we disagree with you does not mean we are sexist. Being a politically active woman with strong feminist values does not mean that everything you say is right!"

After the outburst the conversation becomes more civil and the volume is lowered and we all share ideas and I feel enriched. I feel privileged to be among the leaders of an honest-to-goodness revolution that has changed lives and the lives of countless people to come.

Then, just when I think I understand the women's movement and, more important, can actually make a contribution to it, and just when I feel the excitement of knowing that my "male views" are being taken seriously by some women on the front lines, someone in the office will say, "Marlo on line two," and I will seize the phone eagerly and say, "Hi, honey!" and her secretary will say, "Just a moment for Marlo," and I will be pissed off all over again.

19

The Gatekeepers

TELEVISION IS a business controlled by men (seldom women) who are, in effect, the Gatekeepers. These men decide what and who gets on America's living-room screens. Their profits allow them to play a giant chess game with enormously expensive programs in a Super Bowl environment that will determine a "winner" and a "loser" in any given time period. Meanwhile, "the people," those wonderful folks who turn up on the TV general manager's desk in the form of a number in a Nielsen rating book, are not only kept out of any decision making: they are kept out of the TV station as well.

Concern about "kooks" and terrorists has turned most of this country's TV stations into forts, with uniformed security personnel and electronic buzzers that admit only card-carrying people beyond the lobby. While TV's anxiety about security is understandable, its increased protectiveness has served to remove it even further from the communities whose "interest" the FCC obliges the license holder to serve. And while television executives understand America's theory of regulated broadcasting (airwaves owned by the people; daily control licensed to the operator), TV's management people nevertheless think of the station, the employees, the programs, the tower and *the airwaves* as "mine."

The faces America sees on television, both local and national, are there because they passed tests administered by the Gatekeepers. The tests check the applicant's appearance, sense of humor, eye contact, motor activity (especially important for game-show contestants), warmth (especially important for newscasters). Except for lip service to the need for "innovation," there is very little enthusiasm for "different" ideas. The Gatekeepers have a good thing going, and there is very little interest in "different drummers" or "boat rocking." Let's just keep the game-show hosts toothy, the contestants well screened and animated, the newscasters warm, and my God, how the money rolls in!

Most of all, let's keep the people out of here. There is a disdain for the "public" along the hallways of broadcasting's executive-row carpet land. And while studio audiences are "permitted" to watch some sitcoms, game shows and talk shows, we almost never see them, except for occasional shots of the backs of their heads. If baseball pitchers have a "book" on opposing batters (high and tight, low and away), then surely TV programmers have a "book" on the public (dumb and uninteresting).

How else can we explain applause signs and laugh tracks and ten-second audience-waving segments on talk shows? Television has become an "I-thou" medium, and the "I's" not only have it, they own it, lock, stock and airwaves. And the Gatekeepers are going to be very careful about whom they let in.

The result is a closed system that breeds a copycat programming strategy which gives us "soaps and games" in the daytime and "spin-offs" and clones at night. Thus, if *Charlie's Angels* works, why not try *Flying High?* (Lenny Bruce said the reason novelty stores sell plastic puke is because the shit did so well.) The bottom line is profit, not creative opportunity. The Tube is a vehicle for selling things, not for exploring new ideas.

Basketball coaches live with the constant anxiety that in a crucial situation their best player may, as the result of the decision of the coach himself, be on the bench. So today's television viewer might wonder, as he watches the blandness of today's TV offering, whether the best TV talent might be on the bench, or in the mail room or driving the bus, simply because he or she failed to pass the conformity tests offered by the powerful men who stand at the gates of America's multibillion-dollar television business, deciding who gets in and who doesn't.

It took ten years on the air before the *Donahue* show finally "got in," and even today our program is occasionally stopped at the "gate." Our program was not born in New York or Los Angeles, nor was it encouraged by the powerful men in both those media centers, men who can, with the wave of a hand, make or break a career or a program.

For almost a decade *The Phil Donahue Show* struggled without the endorsement of these television kingmakers. Finally, in 1976 *Donahue* was purchased by the Multimedia Corporation of Greenville, South Carolina, for $425,000. The program at the time of the purchase was airing in approximately 45 cities and appeared to be going nowhere. We had moved to Chicago the year before in the hope of attracting better guests, and the man in charge of selling the program on the road had just resigned with the urgent counsel that "the show needs major surgery." Multimedia's acquisition of *Donahue* was an afterthought, an asterisk to a bigger deal that involved purchase of WLWT in Cincinnati, the flagship station of the once-proud Avco Broadcasting Corporation.

The parent Avco Corporation, a conglomerate, had gotten itself into financial trouble with a very expensive and very unsuccessful venture into home video entertainment. The $50-million loss forced the giant company to sell its entire broadcast division. And so onto the auction block went not only the Cincinnati station, but the Dayton station (the *Donahue* home for six years), and three other TV stations.

The *Donahue* show was not a main item in any of the multimillion-dollar negotiations regarding Avco properties; it was a coattailer. Our "home" in Dayton (WLW-D) was purchased by Grinnell College in Iowa for $12 million. Three years later, a national magazine speculated (with good authority) that the resale value of the building, the cameras, the office equipment, the wrestler's dressing room, was $35 million. In three years Grinnell had tripled its investment.

Sadly, it has not tripled its local live programming. Channel 2 in Dayton (now WDTN-TV) has ended the long tradition of local programming pioneered by the original owner, Powell Crosley. After *Donahue* moved to Chicago, the local program that replaced it was canceled in order to make room for an expanded (to ninety minutes) network soap opera.

And the studios of the NBC affiliate in Dayton, the place where thousands cheered while area wrestlers took the count and where thousands more looked on and even participated in almost 2,000 *Donahue* programs—that same place is now, like so many churches, almost always dark and empty.

The Dayton/Grinnell situation is just a microcosm of what has happened to America's most influential twentieth-century invention. While the people who manage Grinnell College's investment portfolio take bows for their business acumen, there is no apparent interest in ensuring that their "property" is being used to provide a platform for local civic personalities. Nor is there any apparent interest in providing opportunities for new talent and fresh faces to be recognized and encouraged. We can only speculate on where Doris Day, Andy Williams, Rosemary Clooney and others like them would have gone had they had the misfortune of trying to be discovered in Dayton today. As each local television program fades, to be replaced by network reruns, the industry's minor leagues diminish and the power of the Gatekeepers in New York and Los Angeles grows more ominous. No more Triple A, just Big Leagues.

With the end of local live programming on Channel 2 in Dayton came the end of an era. Somewhere in Dayton, Ohio, there may be a young man or woman with talent, a large vocabulary and a healthy enthusiasm for creative and innovative television programming. That person is not likely to have an opportunity to express those gifts because the Gatekeepers, owners of a $35-million television station, have, in the interest of profits, chosen to accept the expanded programming material offered by the network. And while the lights are out in the old *Donahue* studio on South Dixie Drive, Daytonians are now able to watch another thirty minutes of *Another World*.

20

The Grotto

RECENTLY DURING a visit to Notre Dame, I walked alone to the Grotto. I stared at the stone and the statue, and at the candles and the railing before which thousands of people have knelt, and I thought of how little that sanctuary had changed since my student days. I thought about all those cold South Bend winters and of the evening ritual when we walked to the Grotto on our way back to our dorm after dinner. I thought of all of the members of The Gang who stopped there, dressed in parkas and scarves, heads bowed in prayer. The Grotto was a place of comfort, a place where you could check in with the most important woman in all of Christianity, and where you could ask favors of her, hoping she would take your petition to Her Son:

> Remember, O most gracious Virgin Mary
> That never was it known
> That anyone who fled to thy protection
> Implored thy help
> Or sought thy intercession
> Was left unaided . . .

The Grotto looked so much the same that I was made all the more aware of how much I had changed. I thought of all the intervening years and how so much that was important had not gone as planned. I thought about the other members of The Gang and about how I was the only one who was divorced.

The sun was setting on a beautiful autumn day, and I wondered how I was still on my feet after all this change. I wondered how my values had changed, and whether I was better or worse for having rebelled and walked away from Holy Mother Church. I thought about a college buddy who had inquired recently of another of The Gang, "How come Donahue has all those damn queers on his show?"

I thought about the large psychic void that is left by a loss of faith and of how so many Catholics had tried so many things to replace it: yoga, psychiatry, consciousness groups. I thought about how much I missed the opportunity to sit in an empty church at night and look at the ugly windows (at night you can't see the images in the stained glass, just the lead that holds the pieces in place) and the sanctuary lamp, and the altar boys who used to snuff out the candles after Benediction. And I realized how much I missed the opportunity to ask for favors—passing grades, purity, happy marriage.

> Inspired by this confidence
> I fly unto thee
> O virgin of virgins, my Mother
> To thee I come. Before thee I stand
> Sinful and sorrowful.

I thought about my childhood on Southland Avenue and how I knew the name of the family in every house on the street. And about Christmas, and what a wonderful fantasy it was. And how today, December 25th has become guilt and obligation.

I thought about the immigrants who built all those American Catholic churches and schools while in poverty—and about all those modern Catholics who complain about maintaining them, while in prosperity. I thought of those immigrants of the past, and I wondered what responsibility I have to them.

I thought about the Notre Dame students of my time gathered in Sacred Heart Church, and how exciting the sound of their thousand young male voices had been singing "Holy God, We Praise Thy Name." How proud I had been to be Catholic and at Notre Dame, and how I had sung even louder as the goose bumps crept on. I thought about how easily I would have gone to war after singing with them, and wondered how many Catholics before me actually had.

I thought about Father Smyth and our Theology/Philosophy discussions—and about how he had discovered the capacity for wonder in us. And I thought about how different he was from all the rule givers and insecure Church authoritarians, convinced as they were, that the world was going to hell and rebellious Catholics were leading it there.

I thought about my future and where in this world I was going. And I wondered how the going would be without all the help I had come to enlist as a child. I thought about my "guardian angel" and how comforting it had been to have *her* helping, and about the saints we had had for special favors (St. Anthony to find lost items, St. Blaze to keep throats free of foreign objects, St. Jude to address impossible cases, St. Theresa the Little Flower for purity). I felt the loss not only of my faith, but of all the emotional supports that went with it. There at the Grotto, in my 44th year, I was alone.

I was proud of the waves I had made, but wondered how many boats I was supposed to rock. What about my future? What about my soul?

I thought again about the void and how much harder it is to rebel than to just "go along." And as I did so, my life's contrasts appeared in sharp focus—from knowing what a sin was to wondering whether we had concentrated on the right ones, from being absolutely certain there was a God to being absolutely certain that I wasn't sure, from asking God for all kinds of favors to not treating Him like Santa Claus.

Nowhere else on earth, it seemed, were the contrasts in my life so evident. There was the Grotto, made of stone, immutable. Here was the former student, made of flesh and blood—and doubt.

Never again would I give the Church or any institution the power to make decisions about my moral well-being. Never again would I go to confession for "absolution," and never would I go to a body of strange disinterested men to seek a marriage "annulment." Whereas once I would have baptized a "pagan" child, now I would do all I could to encourage him not to take the rap. Nor would I allow a group of old men (sitting on hard wooden benches in Rome or Trent) to presume to tell me what is a mortal or a venial sin and what is the prescribed punishment for each. Nor would I ever see suffering as a virtue, whether "offered up" or not.

Never again would I pray for the religious "conversion of Russia" or any other country or group of persons. Never again would I allow anyone to claim that God was on any one side during a war. Praising the Lord and passing the ammunition are mutually exclusive ideas.

I had moved, in my forty-three years, from certainty to doubt, from devotion to rebellion. And I knew that after all the Masses, sacraments, novenas and retreats, and even after the anger of activism and the confusion of defeat, I would never completely "lose my faith." A little piece of it would always be there.

And I felt a little sad. I knew there would always be a part of me that would want to go back. I also knew that I never would.

O Mother of the Word Incarnate
Despise not my petition
But in Thy mercy,
Hear and answer me.
Amen.

An October breeze came in off St. Joseph's Lake and washed through the trees around the Grotto, and the candles flickered against the stone wall underneath the statue of Our Lady, Notre Dame.

Acknowledgments

THIS BOOK is about me, and some of the "funny" things that happened to me on the way past TV's Gatekeepers. It is also about the show that we have created. Sharing this experience with me, among others, are seven people from the *Donahue* office in Chicago, who also share in the proceeds of this book and shared in writing parts of it—as well as giving me their support and help. They are the people who began the *Donahue* odyssey from an "office" that had served as the wrestlers' dressing room when "live" Saturday programming in Dayton in the fifties meant a match between Mickey the Mansfield Mauler and Terrible Tomahawk the Insane Indian. Executive Producer Dick Mincer, Senior Producer Patricia McMillen, Producer Darlene Hayes and I will all share equally in the revenue of this book and all related income. Also sharing (but at a lesser percentage) are four other *Donahue* laborers who joined our "family" at a later date: Producer Sheri Singer, Publicity Director Penny Rotheiser, Director Ron Weiner and our long-suffering and eternally helpful and optimistic secretary, Lorraine Landelius.

A special thanks also to the untiring efforts of the other *Donahue* staffers, Dorothy Ghallab, Lillian Smith, Marilyn O'Reilly, Cindy Kenyon, Joycelyn Marnul, Joe DiCanio, Wendy Roth, Mike Brown, Jennie Rayls and Mason Harris.

Except for the Staff chapter, I wrote this book myself—a fact that came as no surprise to my editor, Michael Korda, who enthusiastically did what he could with what he had, and never once sounded paternalistic or condescending.

A special thanks to my literary agent, Bill Adler, who came to Chicago and over a beer in a bar in the Loop proposed this book. It should also be noted that his proposal came B.N.Y.—before our show succeeded in New York.

Many thanks to Paul and Mary Lou Reisinger, the best Catholics I know, who were the first to read the manuscript and offer me their advice ("Please take out the dirty words") and their love and best wishes for success.

My gratitude goes also to Hazel Dyer, who worked for us in Dayton, and whose "presence" will always be felt in our office. To Deanne Mincer, my thanks for her painstaking review of this manuscript and her suggested changes.

To our lawyer, William Maddux, and our financial consultant, Sam Roberman, "Donahue & Co." says Thank you, for the instruments which define our agreement with each other regarding the revenue from this book and for making this complicated assignment understandable—a fact which ensures that no matter what happens with this project, it will not alter the love and respect we have for each other . . . now and always.

Photography Credits

(Numbers denote pictures in photo sections.)